PROVE THEM WRONG

The Kids Who Refused to Quit

By

Nancy K. Shugart

Copyright © 2010
By Nancy K. Shugart

All Rights Reserved. No part of this book may be reproduced or utilized in any form or by any means, electronic or mechanical, including photocopying, recording or by information storage or retrieval system, without permission in writing from the publisher.

ISBN: 978-0-9846094-0-6

Published by
Prove Them Wrong
6705 Hwy 290 West
Suite 502-148
Austin, TX 78749
866-733-5157
www.ProveThemWrong.com

Table of Contents

What People Are Saying About This Book   1

Foreword by Erik Weihenmayer   5

1. It Happened Because I Wanted It to Happen   9
   Jesus Bautista

2. I Set Out to Prove Her Wrong   17
   Remy Ceballos

3. Don't Let Anyone Tell You That You Can't Make   23
   Your Dreams Come True
   John V. Wright, Jr.

4. Keep Your Nose in the Window   31
   Paul Orfalea

5. Tough Love   35
   Regina Blye

6. Challenge the Naysayers   41
   Miguel Aguayo

7. I Followed My Own Plan, Not Theirs   49
   Sarah Stup

8. I Could Become a Voice   57
   Tony Volpentest

9. They Make Us Prevail   61
     Laurel Marshall

10. From the Mundane to the Extraordinary   71
     Geerat Vermeij

11. My Eyes Are on the Finish Line and I'm   81
     Not Stopping Until I Get There
     Kelly Sutton

12. I Realized I Was Okay   89
     Doug Grady

13. Undaunted Determination   95
     Sheri Denkensohn

14. I Couldn't, but I Could   103
     Tony Melendez

15. I Don't Waste the Energy   113
     Kathryn Woodcock

16. Keep Focusing on the Top of Your Mountain   117
     Richard Turner

17. It Fueled My Fire to Become the Best I Felt   127
     I Could Become
     Chris Glavin

18. I Just Went Ahead with My Plan   131
     Betty Davidson

19. Surround Yourself with Smart People   139
     David Pierce

20. I Took Advantage of Every Opportunity   147
     Thrown at Me
     Erik Weihenmayer

A Note from the Publisher	157
Tell Us Your Story	159
About the Author	161
Resources	163

What People Are Saying About This Book

"There is a human inclination to identify with others through stories of overcoming challenges. *Prove Them Wrong: The Kids Who Refused to Quit*, a wonderful collection of such stories, can give any reader the assurance that they can deal with anything that comes their way. Any child with a disability will feel more empowered – I think everyone should read this book."

   -Chet Cooper, Publisher, Ability Magazine, and Founder, Ability Corps, www.AbilityMagazine.com

"Reading *Prove Them Wrong: The Kids Who Refused to Quit* made me think of all the potential out there in kids with disabilities. I wish I could put this book in the hands of anyone who's thinking about giving up on a child. This book can bring back hope!"

   -Christian Lindstrom, Director, LD OnLine
   www.LDOnline.org

"There is no greater ability than having a belief in oneself. And no greater gift to give someone else than to foster their belief. *Prove Them Wrong: The Kids Who Refused to Quit* challenges each of us to overcome the barriers that keep us from being all we can be – as individuals, as a community, as a world. It's time to accept that challenge."

   -Joanne Ritter, Director of Marketing and Communications, Guide Dogs for the Blind, Inc., www.GuideDogs.com

www.ProveThemWrong.com

"'Don't put any limits on him.' This was the best advice someone gave me about my son who has autism. Not only will you hear this advice throughout *Prove Them Wrong: The Kids Who Refused to Quit*, but you'll witness first-hand in these stories what happens when this advice is heeded."

-Peter McNabb, Vice President & General Manager, USA News Network, www.USANewsNetwork.com

"It is amazing to read these stories of triumph. It shows what can be accomplished in the face of adversity. The stories in *Prove Them Wrong: The Kids Who Refused to Quit* should encourage everyone to climb as high as they can."

-Lynn Bozof, President, National Meningitis Association, www.NMAUS.org

"In a word, inspirational! These portraits of determination in the face of adversity remind us of the incredible potential in every human being. Young readers, whether or not they are facing blindness or other disabilities, are sure to be inspired and motivated by these true stories of young people overcoming seemingly insurmountable obstacles."

-Andrew Jackson, Director of Communications, Glaucoma Research Foundation, www.glaucoma.org

"*Prove Them Wrong: The Kids Who Refused to Quit* is a great tool to empower people with disabilities to take action on their plans and dreams for their lives. Regardless of the disability, the people in this book achieved what most had said would be impossible."

-Corey Hudson, CEO, Canine Companions for Independence, www.CCI.org

"*Prove Them Wrong: The Kids Who Refused to Quit* is more evidence of what we in the blindness field already know – every day, people with disabilities not only live and work successfully alongside their non-disabled peers, but also strive for and achieve remarkable feats. For those who don't yet know this, or for anyone, disabled or not, who has ever been told, 'You can't,' I urge you to read this book. These stories will change your attitude about the capabilities and capacity of young people with disabilities to dream big and do more than anyone thought possible."

- Carl R. Augusto, President & CEO, American Foundation for the Blind, www.AFB.org

"Freedom. Independence. Courage. Tenacity. These are themes that permeate *Prove Them Wrong: The Kids Who Refused to Quit*. As we are inspired by our clients, you will be inspired by the stories in this book. Read on!"

-Jack Hayward, Director of Communications, The Fidelco Guide Dog Foundation, Inc., www.Fidelco.org

"Showcasing the strength of the human spirit, these stories bring disability down to a very human, one-on-one level with the reader. Engaging text illuminates, in simple terms, the tragedies and triumphs of a host of real-life heroes. Every story left me wanting to read more."

-Debbie Marsh, Editor, Disaboom, Inc., www.Disaboom.com

www.ProveThemWrong.com

Foreword

In 2008, I completed my quest to climb the "Seven Summits," the tallest peak on every continent. For a blind person, climbing mountains has been an unusual path to say the least. I'm fortunate to live an exciting and fulfilling life, full of adventure, but my journey began in a similar way to the kids featured in the stories you are about to read.

As a young teenager, I began to lose the last traces of my sight. I could no longer walk around by myself, so my brothers and parents had to lead me. I hated what was happening. Blindness was like a storm descending upon me with such force, I thought I might be crushed by it.

Just before I lost my sight entirely, I was watching a TV show called *That's Incredible*. I could still see a little out of one eye, although I had to crane forward a few inches away from the screen. Featured on the program that night was an amazing athlete named Terry Fox. Terry had lost a leg to cancer and, not yet discharged from the hospital, made a bold decision to run across Canada from east to west. Many people would have shrunk under the weight of this tragedy, but Terry did the complete opposite; he squared off with adversity and ran into its very midst.

With my nose pressed against the TV screen, and with tears rolling down my face, I watched Terry run. The thousands of miles took a tremendous toll on his amputated leg and primitive prosthetic. He hobbled along mile after mile, fighting the pain of blisters and raw skin.

What struck me the most was the look on Terry's face. It was a look of extreme contradiction: full of exhaustion yet radiant with exultation. In his thin face was the trace flicker of an intense internal light that burned power into his struggling frame. That light seemed to actually feed on adversity, to consume it like fuel. The bigger the challenge, the brighter that light burned. I wondered if that light burned in me. Could I use it to become more focused, more determined, more creative? Could I use that light to transcend my own limitations to give my life purpose? The image filled my sagging spirit and gave me a feeling of utter courage. It was while staring into Terry's face that I first wondered how we could turn into the storm and emerge on the other side, not just undamaged, but stronger and better.

Since seeing Terry on TV, I've met many others like him. I call people like Terry, alchemists. They take the lead that life continually piles on top of them and find a way to turn it into gold. An alchemist doesn't just deal well with adversity. They actually take it a step further. They find a way to seize hold of that storm of adversity which swirls around us, to harness its energy, and use its force to propel themselves to places they might not have gone to in any other way. These people see obstacles not as a deterrent, but as the pathway to growth, innovation, and pioneering achievements.

Prove Them Wrong: The Kids Who Refused to Quit is a book about alchemy. How did a child whom medical experts labeled severely brain-damaged grow up to earn two college degrees and become a meteorologist? How did a teenaged girl who lost her foot in an accident grow up to use her engineering skills to assist others to walk? How did a young boy who could not communicate in the traditional manner grow up to build a successful business that allows television to communicate to millions worldwide? From engineers to educators, from Olympic gold medalists to professional athletes, from scientists and inventors to acclaimed entertainers, from attorneys and authors to highly trained specialists, and from leaders of businesses to leaders who leave a legacy, the kids you will read about in this book have blasted through others' expectations to make a major mark on our nation and the world.

The kids who refused to quit are not extra-ordinary. They do not possess supernatural powers. They are not born with an internal

GPS unit steering them away from barriers. In fact, it's just the opposite. Every young person in this book faced barriers so enormous that, to just about everyone watching, it seemed they had no choice but to give up on their life dreams. So why didn't they quit? When many youth who have a disability are not completing high school, why did the young people featured in this book refuse to quit? When the majority of adults who have a disability are underemployed or unemployed, how did the adults you will read about in this book achieve successful employment? What do they know that the majority of their counterparts do not know?

A Chinese proverb says, "To know the road ahead, ask those coming back." Every person in this book is coming back. They have been down that road that every young person is about to travel. They will tell you what they have discovered on their journey. They will teach you lessons of risk-taking, of unshakeable perseverance, and you will have the rare privilege to journey with them as they climb higher than anyone dreamed possible.

– Erik Weihenmayer

"Courage is the capacity to hear what others say is impossible and believe you are the one to make it happen."

– Nancy Shugart, Owner, Prove Them Wrong

www.ProveThemWrong.com

1
It Happened Because I Wanted It to Happen
Jesus Bautista

Jesus was growing up in the Second Ward, or Segundo Barrio, a very low income area in El Paso, Texas. His family lived in a three-room apartment which had no bathroom – only a living room, dining room and kitchen. Jesus, his two brothers, his five sisters, and his mother and father called these cramped quarters home.

At night the three rooms were turned into make-shift bedrooms. Jesus and his brothers slept in the living room and his sisters in the dining room. The kitchen, with the addition of a roll-away bed, doubled as the parents' bedroom.

There was a flurry of activity each morning as children and parents from every apartment in the complex scrambled for a chance to use one of the three community bathrooms in a separate building from where his family's apartment was.

Once at school, the children were required to speak English instead of their parents' language, Spanish. Jesus loved to learn and he loved learning English. However, he had been born with coloboma, a rare eye disease that left him permanently visually impaired. To see to read, he had to hold the book very close to his face. He knew the spelling of the words, but his eyes couldn't make out the letters, and he would stumble through the sentences.

"After a while," Jesus said, "my teachers just stopped calling on me during classroom activities. They didn't think I could read and I slowed them down too much."

Increasingly, Jesus was left out of more classroom and school activities. However, his parents refused to treat him any differently from their other seven children. He began working when he was nine years old, shining shoes and selling newspapers.

"My parents knew I would have to make my way in the world," Jesus said, "and so they treated me just like any other kid."

The public school he was attending, however, was finding it difficult to treat Jesus like the other students. He was struggling to see to read, and so it took him longer to complete assignments. Finally, they advised his parents to enroll their son in the School for the Blind.

"No way," was his mother's reaction. She refused to accept that her son could not be educated in the same classroom with children who could see.

At the end of Jesus's second grade year, his parents withdrew him from that school and, desperate to provide their son with a quality education, enrolled him in a Catholic school when he began third grade. This was an extra expense that they struggled to manage, making only minimal payments whenever they could.

But things did not change. His new teachers, unequipped to teach their only student who had a visual impairment, resorted to the same tactics as their public school counterparts – ignoring him.

"I felt alone. I felt left out," Jesus said.

Though Jesus loved to learn, he didn't love school. He was excluded from most activities at school since his teachers believed he could not see well enough to participate.

"I was left out of everything at school," Jesus said, "and so I had a lot of time to get into trouble. Kids who were seen as being weak were the ones who were always getting picked on, and I was that kid in El Paso."

Schoolyard fights landed Jesus in the principal's office on a regular basis. To make matters worse, his parents had fallen so far behind in their payments to the Catholic school that they were asked to withdraw Jesus from the school. This was a major turning point as Jesus approached his eighth grade year.

His parents, knowing their son was headed for a life of trouble if he didn't get a good education, knew they had to make a change. "Had I not gotten out of that environment," Jesus said, "I believe I would have ended up dead or in jail."

His mom and dad moved the family nine miles west of El Paso to Sunland Park, New Mexico. But this would not be Jesus's new home. His parents enrolled Jesus in the New Mexico School for the Blind in Alamogordo, New Mexico, which was nearly 100 miles from their new home. Jesus, just barely thirteen years old, was now living in a dormitory at his new school.

"I cried myself to sleep every night for the first few weeks that I was there," Jesus said. "It was so hard to be away from my family."

It was the wrestling coach at this school who would play an enormous role in Jesus's future. This coach, who was also visually impaired, encouraged Jesus to join the wrestling team to help him release some of his energy and distract him from activities that would get him into trouble.

"But I had no interest in wrestling," Jesus admitted. "I wanted to play basketball and football like the other boys." Jesus laughed as he added, "But I was no dummy. I noticed I got hit by the ball more than anyone else."

He finally decided to accept the wrestling coach's invitation to join the wrestling team. His world began to turn around. He worked hard and his hard work was rewarded with success, both as an athlete and now also as a student.

He graduated from high school and then he did something that no one in his family had ever done – he went to college. His parents, who had very little education, could not have been more proud. Jesus was the only one of their eight children with a visual impairment, and it was a dream come true to see him being accepted into college. His parents, who had been told countless times that he could never succeed, now believed that their son was on his way to a life of success.

Jesus remembers how angry his mother would get when his well-meaning uncles, who stopped by the house frequently, would tell her that Jesus would never be able to make anything of himself. She would answer, "Not this one. He's a go-getter."

"She would get so angry," Jesus said. "She refused to give up on me. She always believed I could do anything any other kid could do. And I wasn't about to let her down. I always took a lot of pride in my family's name. My parents set a goal for me and I wasn't about to quit. Quitting was not in our family's vocabulary."

After graduating from New Mexico Highlands University with a degree in education, he went on to teach language arts to high school special education students in New Mexico, and later returned to teach in the public schools in El Paso, Texas. But few noticed Mr. Bautista as he would move through the busy hallways at Irvin High

School. That's because the attention would go to his four-legged companion, Bishop, a graduate from Guide Dogs for the Blind.

Students respectfully ignored Bishop so as not to distract him from doing his job, but the presence of this adorable Golden Retriever would always bring a smile to everyone's face as they passed him in the hallway.

Mr. Bautista not only taught full-time but he also served as the high school's wrestling coach for both the girls' and boys' wrestling teams. Many of these wrestling students proudly won individual state championships under Coach Bautista's direction. And Guide Dog Bishop also became a familiar face as he traveled with Coach Bautista to wrestling tournaments around the state of Texas.

Mr. Bautista retired from his 32-year teaching career in 2009. He accomplished a lot as a teacher and coach in the public schools. He used himself as a model for his students. Though most of his students were not visually impaired, they looked at their teacher who was blind and believed that if he could succeed, then maybe they could, too.

"I was very fortunate to have had the opportunity to work with students who have a disability," Mr. Bautista says. "I took great pride in their accomplishments. I would say that my teaching career has been a very rewarding gift."

Mr. Bautista's influence on students has not been limited to his own students. He received an appointment from the Texas governor to serve as a member of the school board of the Texas School for the Blind and Visually Impaired, where he served for eight years.

Mr. Bautista will tell you, "I believe the main key to my success has been persistence, the unwillingness to ever give up."

He also believes that he has had some very good people in his life who have encouraged him, including teachers, coaches, his mother, and, during his adult life, his wife, Lorenza.

Mr. Bautista has not only earned the admiration of his students but also that of his family and friends. He and his wife of more than thirty-five

years are the proud parents of three sons and four grandchildren. Their three sons all have impressive accomplishments of their own. One is a successful business owner, one is the head wrestling coach at a Texas high school, and one is a pilot!

Their eldest son told them one day that what he learned from his parents was that failure was never an option. Mr. Bautista said that was exactly what he had learned from his own parents, who had faced many hardships and had immigrated to the United States from Mexico.

Mr. Bautista believes that his greatest accomplishment is that he became successful as a man, as a coach, and as a father.

He says, "You should not allow people to determine your future for you. You have to have the will to succeed. You have to have the will to make mistakes and recover from those. You know in your heart whether or not you want to be somebody and the only one that can make that determination is you.

"When I was in junior high I had a teacher who told me that I would never amount to anything. Well, since then I have become a successful college graduate. I married and have a beautiful wife and three kids. I became a successful teacher, a successful coach, and that didn't happen because somebody told me I was going to be able to do that.

"It happened because I wanted it to happen. Success comes in different modes. You are the only one who can determine that."

"Follow your passion. Follow your heart.
They will lead you to the place you want to go."

– Evelyn Glennie, solo percussionist who is deaf.

www.evelyn.co.uk

2
I Set Out to Prove Her Wrong
Remy Ceballos

It was summertime in San Leandro, California, a small town about twenty-two miles from San Francisco. Remy remembers that fateful summer day. "When I was fifteen years old, I was in ninth grade summer school and I was walking home with my friend. There was a Southern Pacific train, over three quarters of a mile long, cars all combined, which had stopped on the track. It had been stopped for about thirty minutes.

"I could see my house, about fifty yards away. Being young and impatient, we decided to walk across the tracks. It was a shortcut everyone took. That day, a group of boys down the way were crossing, and up ahead, some other girls were crossing.

"My friend had hopped over the top of the train and it was fairly high and she needed to get down. With me being kind of shorter, I ducked under the coupling of the train to help her down. But this train began to move without any notice."

As the two girls were trying to run away from the train, the corner of Remy's baggy jeans got caught on the railing and the train ended up running over Remy's right foot, slicing it off just above the ankle.

"I can remember that day," Remy says, thinking back to that painful turning point in her life. "I can remember lying there just hoping this was a dream. 'I'm going to wake up.' And thinking, 'If I don't wake up then my life is over. I'm never going to be the same person that I was. I'll never live the same life. I'm going to be in a wheelchair for the rest of my life.'"

Remy did go home from the hospital in a wheelchair. This teenaged girl now faced the difficult task of being fitted for an artificial limb. The first one Remy was fitted with was terribly uncomfortable to wear, extremely stiff, and walking on it was awkward.

So many changes had occurred in her life in such a very short period of time. She had to adjust to having an artificial limb and to the limited mobility she felt she now had. This once very confident young girl began to notice something changing inside her. She said, "You know, before I lost my foot, I felt that there was nothing in the world I couldn't do. But then after the accident, my self-esteem and my confidence was severely reduced."

Remy had to decide if she was going to continue to be strong and pursue her dreams in life or if she was going to just quit. It would be the words of a doctor that would help Remy to make this decision.

Remy said, "I can recall a doctor telling me shortly after the accident that I would never walk without the use of crutches or a cane, and I just refused to accept that. It was almost as if her words had the opposite effect on me, and I set out to prove her wrong! Those words just pushed me into gear. I said, 'You know what, I refuse to accept that.'"

By the time Remy graduated from high school, she was one determined young lady who was daring to dream extraordinary dreams. She began by doing something that no one in her family had ever done – she enrolled in college. It wasn't easy. With the enormous cost of tuition, Remy worked, often full-time, while taking a full load of classes.

www.ProveThemWrong.com

She married and soon their family began to grow. First one beautiful daughter and then, two years later, a second beautiful daughter was born to them.

No matter how busy Remy was with family, school, and work, she never lost sight of her mission. Her mission since being fitted with the first artificial limb had been to figure out a way to develop a better prosthetic leg.

At a technology conference at DeVry University, Remy won first place with her senior project, which was an electronically-controlled prosthetic foot. Remy said, "That was what got my first exposure to the world of who I am. From that day on I set out to improve that field of prosthetics. I felt that so much more could be done in this field. And from that day on I set out to do so."

This headstrong young woman, who is African-American, then went on to earn her Bachelor of Science degree in electronics engineering technology from Fremont's DeVry University, a degree that is not commonly earned by women or those from minority groups.

Soon after graduating, Remy began her career as an electronics technologist for Livermore National Laboratory.

She said, "It was an awesome opportunity. I got to work with some of the brightest scientists, physicists, and engineers in the world. I had direct exposure to some of the latest technology. That's what I loved most about that job.

"You know, after I graduated I chose to take that opportunity because I felt that it was not only a great opportunity, but it also helped me to develop a huge array of electronic skills. And that was my goal as I started into the field of prosthetics, was to really enhance the electronic aspects of it. In that position at Lawrence Livermore, I was exposed to a huge array of knowledge. It's still my lifetime goal to design electronically-controlled prosthetics, and the laboratory actually gave me access to that. It was like a tech wonderland – tech Disneyland – anything I could possibly dream of was at my fingertips.

"The great thing about being there was that I was not just working in one field. I didn't just work with software or hardware. I actually worked in a research and development environment, protecting national security and improving gene projects and all kinds of wonderful things going on at Lawrence Livermore. And we had the technology to apply great science to those fields to advance them. And my job as an electronics technologist has been to build the devices and develop the devices that actually aid in applying these new technologies that were created there."

After several years at Lawrence Livermore, Remy accepted a position as project engineer for Monster Cable, Inc. Remy said, "This was a matter of leaving my comfort zone and taking a more challenging position that would allow me to grow career-wise. I was honored that Monster had sought me out and thought I would be a valuable asset to their company. In my new position, I am travelling the world, meeting executives and celebrities, and truly enjoying what I do."

Is this the same person as the young teenaged girl who thought her life was over after the accident? The contrast of Remy as a teenager and Remy as an adult could not be more pronounced. But she is the same person. She is living proof of what happens when a teenager who is faced with seemingly insurmountable odds refuses to give up.

Remy's enthusiasm is contagious as she adds, "To be where I am today from that day, lying there on the side of the track, I feel that I have more than accomplished my goals in life."

"The key for me is believing in myself. If I believe in myself, every time someone else says I can't do it, it just fuels me to believe harder and push stronger for what I'm trying to achieve. I never take no for an answer. If I would settle, I would not be where I am.

If I didn't think that I could go to school as a parent and multi-task family and career – if I didn't believe in that, I wouldn't be where I am.

"Don't be afraid of change. No matter how difficult or unobtainable you might think your dreams are, go for them! Regardless of the outcome, you will become a better person for having taken the risk."

"I challenge you to go through a single day exploring every aspect, not from what is realistic, but instead from what is possible."

– Jim Stovall, founder and president of Narrative Television Network

www.NarrativeTV.com

3
Don't Let Anyone Tell You That You Can't Make Your Dreams Come True
John V. Wright, Jr.

It was Christmas Day, 1957. John, like a typical eleven-year-old boy, awoke with great excitement. He knew and believed in the true meaning of Christmas. He also knew that this was a day when presents were shared, and he had been begging his parents to give him a bicycle – his very first bicycle.

John's father was a career military man, a commanding officer in the U.S. Air Force. Like many children who have a parent in the military, John was used to moving a lot – changing homes, changing schools, changing friends.

Waking up on this cold Christmas morning in their Spangdahlem Air Force Base home in western Germany, John raced his younger brother and sister to the living room with expectations of finding three bicycles. Each would probably be of a different color. But one thing would be for sure, John's bike would be the biggest, since he was the oldest. But to John's bitter disappointment, there were only two bicycles sitting in the middle of the room. The sizes of the bikes indicated that neither was meant for John.

Seeing John's obvious disappointment, his mother stepped in. "John," she said, smiling, "we have a very special gift for you." Bringing a very large tricycle into the room, John's parents presented it to their oldest son who, by now, was quite upset.

"A tricycle?" was John's angry response. "I'm eleven years old. I'm not a baby. I don't want a tricycle."

"But John," his mother tried to console him, "you are different. You could get hurt on a bicycle."

Different. Not the same as others. Words that John had heard for as long as he could remember.

* * *

"Your son has cerebral palsy," the doctor at the Warner-Robbins Air Force Base hospital in Macon, Georgia had explained to John's parents soon after he was born. The news stunned John's parents. Though they had heard of CP, as it is commonly called, they knew very little about it.

They learned that CP is the result of damage being done to the developing brain, often due to a lack of oxygen for the baby before and during birth. In John's case, it is believed that the doctor, using forceps during John's delivery, applied too much force to his head, causing the flow of oxygen to be interrupted.

There are many levels of CP, ranging from very mild to very severe, depending on which areas of the brain were damaged and by how much. "Your son's brain damage is so severe," the doctor spelled out in no uncertain terms, "he is not going to live."

Several weeks passed. Finally, the diagnosis was changed. "It appears your son will live," the doctor paused, "but he will never be able to walk."

John's father was stationed at several different Air Force bases around the world during John's childhood. The doctors at these different bases suggested a variety of methods to help John learn to use his muscles. At age four, John was fitted with large leg braces. It was hard to walk with them, but without the braces it was impossible for John to control his leg muscles. Due to the leg braces, John was not allowed to start school with the rest of the kids his age. He was held back one year.

"I really did not begin to walk until the braces came off when I was eight years old," John remembers. "That's when it became much easier to walk."

Another doctor advised John's parents to let him learn to bowl to help him develop his eye-hand coordination. Bowling would soon become one of John's favorite sports. The attention that had been invested in improving John's muscle coordination was paying off.

Now it was time to assist him with his speech. "I took speech therapy for four years beginning when I was nine years old," John remembers. "I could not make my tongue move right to make the words."

Learning to walk and learning to speak are natural processes for most children. But John's childhood was consumed with therapy sessions to teach him what others learned with little effort.

Though the areas of John's brain that were damaged involved his speech and movement, it was becoming obvious that his intelligence had not suffered any damage. As early as age six, John was showing exceptional interest in meteorology.

"I was fascinated with weather," John recalls with excitement in his voice. "As a young child I had one dream over and over again in which I was working in a weather service office. I knew when I grew up that I would work as a meteorologist. No one could take my interest in weather away from me. Because I lived in so many different places during my childhood, I got to experience a lot of different types of weather."

* * *

But on this Christmas day, eleven-year-old John was focused on the unquestionably rotten present waiting for him in the middle of the living room. Should he just quit? Give up? Throw in the towel?

After all, if he was too brain-damaged to ride a bicycle, could he ever expect to be successful in anything?

He had an idea. He took this unusually gigantic tricycle over to the park where he knew he would find kids riding their bicycles. Curiosity about this tricycle soon spread. Kids of all ages began begging John to let them ride his three-wheeler. "Okay," John answered slowly, "but only if you let me ride your bike."

Everyone said yes! John spent many satisfied hours riding the other kids' bikes around that park.

At the end of John's sixth grade year, he and his family moved back to the United States to live in Lake Charles, Louisiana. This city in southwestern Louisiana, just thirty miles upstream from the Gulf of Mexico, would be his home as he completed his last two years of junior high school. It was while living there that John persuaded his dad to get him a weather station. The wet, warm climate, very different from the weather in Germany, gave John new weather variations to explore, especially during hurricane season.

John loved school. He attended public school, surrounded with classmates who did not have a disability, and he could outperform every one of them in his favorite subjects.

"I especially loved math and, of course, science," John says, and he adds, "I would win all of the math contests at school. There finally came a time when the teachers wouldn't let me compete in the contests because I could calculate the problems in my head before the other kids could even begin to start figuring out the answers."

When he completed his eighth grade year, it was time to move again… this time to the Philippines. An island country in Southeast Asia, the Philippines is located in the western Pacific Ocean. "It was great!" John said. "Now I could study tropical weather including the typhoons that came around every year."

While in high school, his home was across the street from a golf course. John watched the golfers with increasing curiosity. Henry, the local golf pro, agreed to see if he could teach a kid with CP to play golf. He did! Two years later, in the tenth grade, John tried out for his high school golf team. He made the team on his first try! "I practiced every day, whether it rained or not." John said, "If I'm going to do something, I'm going to do it well."

At one game, while on the course playing against a rival team, a member of the other team came to John and asked, "How do you do it? I mean, how do you play golf so well?" Without missing a beat, John answered, "The ball doesn't know I have CP."

Upon graduating from high school in the Philippines, John's family moved again, this time to San Angelo, Texas. John attended Angelo State University for one year while deciding where he really wanted to go to college. The next year John was accepted at Texas A&M University.

One of the first things this determined college student did was to buy himself a bicycle – his very first bike – to help him get across the huge campus. Soon after arriving at Texas A&M, John competed for a spot on the university's six-member intercollegiate bowling team and, like with golf, he made the team on his first try. He went on to earn four varsity letters as well as to serve as the team's captain all four years.

Once believed to be too disabled to even ride a bicycle, this young man was now being recognized as an accomplished athlete. In addition, the excellent physical condition John was in helped to boost his endurance level for his studies. But despite his many successes in college, there was one area in which John had little confidence: public speaking – something meteorologists are often called upon to do.

"I used my CP as an excuse not to take speech class in college," John remembers. "Public speaking scared me more than anything."

Though too scared to take speech in college, he was not too scared to tackle the rigorous coursework required for becoming a meteorologist. John went on to earn both a Bachelor of Science and a Master of Science degree in meteorology from Texas A&M University.

Despite holding a master's degree, his supervisor at his first meteorology position was uncomfortable working with someone who had severe muscle spasms. He strongly believed that John would not be able to handle the rigors of the job for which he was hired.

There would be still further roadblocks placed in his path. A promotion was denied him at one job, and he was told at another office not to make any meteorology broadcasts because of his unusual speech.

However, with persistence and hard work, John eventually earned the respect of his bosses and co-workers. His career as a meteorologist was off and running at the National Weather Service, where he worked in many notable positions.

John Wright retired from the National Weather Service in 2006 after living his dream as a meteorologist for thirty-one years. Today he teaches part-time at Virginia Tech University, where he has taught meteorology courses, Einstein's Special Relativity and bowling. He and his wife, Debbie, who is a full-time biochemistry researcher at Virginia Tech, have been married since 1979 and have four children and three grandchildren.

When Mr. Wright is not teaching at the university, he is delivering powerful motivational speeches to audiences across the country. Teaching? Speaking? Yes, all of this from a man who, as a child, struggled to learn to speak and, as a college student, was terrified of public speaking.

Mr. Wright has received innumerable honors, both locally and nationally, for his specialized knowledge in meteorology, his leadership skills, and his work with young people as a role model.

"My key to success is simple," Mr. Wright reveals. "Persevere! My advice to young people is to stay in school. Finish high school and then go to college. Finish college. Get your degree(s). Education is essential to success. And… don't let anyone tell you that you can't make your dreams come true."

For more information about John V. Wright, Jr. and his motivational seminars, visit www.JohnVWrightJr.com.

"Society put labels on me…you're too dumb…
you can't…you won't.
I remember thinking I can change that."

– Kathy Buckley

www.KathyBuckley.com

4
Keep Your Nose in the Window
Paul Orfalea

Paul was born November 28, 1947, and grew up in Los Angeles, California. If his childhood years were any indication of how his life would turn out, it was not a promising picture. He was labeled a hyperactive, dyslexic kid. He flunked the second grade. He couldn't learn the alphabet. Of the eight schools he attended, four expelled him. As his second grade teacher was paddling him, he vowed to himself that one day he would own his own business with a secretary who could read for him.

Paul said, "I may not have been able to read but I could find my way to the principal's office blindfolded. My typical report card came back with two Cs, three Ds, and an F. I graduated from high school with a focus in woodshop, eighth from the bottom of my class of 1,200. Frankly, I still have no idea how those seven kids managed to do worse than I did."

Sometimes, though, being at the bottom can mean the only way left to go is up.

Most kids who graduate from high school at the bottom of their class do not aspire to go to college. Though not yet sure what he wanted to do, and despite the enormous struggles he had faced throughout his school life, Paul went ahead and enrolled in college. As a student at the University of Southern California (USC), he was not at the top of his class, but neither was he at the bottom. A C student, Paul graduated from USC in 1971 with a Bachelor of Science degree in finance.

Was this the same kid who had flunked two grade levels before graduating from high school? Yes, it was.

It was while he was in college that he had an idea – an idea he would eventually grow into a $2 billion business. He noticed that both students and professors needed copies made quickly and at a low cost.

So, in 1970, with a rented copy machine and leased space near the university, Paul founded Kinko's photocopy shops. The name was taken from his curly red hair, and had been his college nickname.

He said, "As someone with a condition I now know is called dyslexia, I could never have predicted I would make my name in what is essentially the reading business."

When Paul Orfalea first started his business, he was told his company would flunk as fast as he had in school. He chose to prove them wrong. He said, "I didn't listen. I knew what I was going to do." There was something else he knew and has lived by ever since. He said, "You don't make a difference in this world by trying to be the same as everyone else."

Within ten years, there were eighty Kinko's stores. But that was just the beginning.

In 2004, Kinko's was acquired by FedEx and rebranded as FedEx Kinko's Office & Print Services. FedEx Kinko's now operates a network of 1,700 locations in eleven countries.

Mr. Orfalea's advice to anyone going after a dream is, "Keep your nose in the window long enough and they are going to let you in."

To see an interview with Paul Orfalea, visit www.youtube.com/watch?v=bJiohyGWZq4

For more information about Paul Orfalea, read his autobiography, which he wrote with Ann Marsh, titled, *Copy This!: Lessons from a Hyperactive Dyslexic Who Turned a Bright Idea Into One of America's Best Companies.*

Visit his website at www.PaulOrfalea.com

"Great spirits have often encountered violent opposition from mediocre minds."

– Albert Einstein

5
Tough Love
Regina Blye

It was a day for celebration. Another school year had come to a close. Regina and her friends were excited about finishing the fourth grade. To celebrate, one of Regina's friends was throwing a slumber party to proclaim the beginning of summer vacation. It was time for fun, friends, and the freedom to run and play in this quiet, small town of Brownfield, located on the South Plains of northwest Texas.

An excited group of young girls began arriving for the much anticipated slumber party. They laughed and chatted incessantly about their lively summer plans. Regina, ten years old, was fired up about the basketball tournament she would be playing in the following week. Anything that involved movement, from climbing trees to playing sports, filled Regina's recreation time.

The girls talked non-stop, not paying much attention to the teenaged brother of the girl giving the party and his friend. However, the brother's friend, thirteen years old, was paying a lot of attention to Regina. He told her that he wanted her to be his girlfriend. "I was only ten years old," Regina said. "I had no interest in boys at that age. All I wanted to do was play outdoors, ride my bike, and compete in basketball games." But the boy persisted.

"I left the room where the party was going on and went into another room to watch TV," Regina remembers. "I was relaxing in the recliner when a strange feeling came over me.

Everything had become uncomfortably silent. I climbed up on my knees and looked over the back of the recliner to see what was going on. That's when I saw the boy standing in the kitchen and pointing a rifle straight at me."

That is the last thing Regina remembers. He pulled the trigger. The bullet hit Regina in the neck.

Before that night would end, Regina's mother would be told by doctors that her baby girl would not live, that it was time to begin making funeral arrangements for her only child.

"At most," the doctor said, "Regina has only a five percent chance of surviving."

The hospital in Regina's small hometown was not equipped to handle such a traumatic injury. She was transferred by helicopter to a larger hospital, forty miles away in Lubbock, Texas. The surgeons were so fearful Regina would die if they used anesthesia, that they performed the surgeries with Regina fully conscious.

The hours turned into days and still Regina held on. As the days turned into weeks, the doctors stopped telling Regina's mother and stepfather that she would die, but instead delivered a sobering diagnosis – quadriplegia.

Their young daughter had some big decisions to make upon learning that she would now be living in a body that was almost completely paralyzed, with only limited use of her hands.

Would she give up? Or would she refuse to quit and be determined to move forward?

"I was so grateful to be alive," Regina said. "I set a goal that I would get out of the hospital in time to be home for Christmas."

She achieved her goal! After being hospitalized since May, Regina arrived home just days before Christmas. Though grateful to be alive and on the road to recovery, she had to learn to do everything all over again, including how to bathe, dress, and feed herself.

"My stepfather was a good man," Regina said. "He worked extra hours so my mother could stay home to help me. She used tough love to teach me. She knew I would have to regain as much independence as possible. She would fix my favorite foods and then coach me on how to eat them. Then she would leave so I would be forced to do it myself."

It was now Regina's fifth grade year. Unable to attend school with her friends, the school sent teachers to her house to do the lessons. For months Regina was unable to speak. To communicate she would blink once for yes and twice for no. Regina said, "I love to talk so much that I would just blink just to be talking!"

The time came when Regina's mother had to return to work. "Because she had to get up very early for work, she was putting me to bed by nine p.m.," Regina said. "'This is not right,' I told her one day. 'I'm eleven years old now. I should be allowed to stay up later.'"

"Okay," Regina's mother answered. "Then you can put yourself to bed."

"Great," Regina thought. But it wasn't so easy. "It took me all night to get myself into bed," Regina laughs as she remembers. "I was so exhausted that next day."

When it was time for Regina to enter middle school, the decision was made to have her return to public school. Regina said, "I was scared. What if the other kids didn't like me any more? They always knew me as someone who played basketball. Now I couldn't play sports any more."

But Regina's vivacious personality had not changed. She was still a lot of fun to be around. It did not matter that she could no longer play basketball. There were plenty of classmates who treasured her friendship.

As Regina grew up she grew into a confident young teenaged girl. "I always felt secure in myself, but my insecurities came when I wondered how others would think of me. In high school there was a boy who said something to me that has stayed with me all of these years. He said, "You have three strikes against you. You are black, female, and in a wheelchair."

"I, however," Regina's smile broadens as she continues, "answered, 'See that not as three strikes but rather as three home runs! Because when people meet me they will never forget me!'"

When you meet Regina you meet a woman whose laughter is contagious and whose determination is unconquerable and unyielding. Quit because she has a disability? No way! When her dream of having a career playing basketball could not come true, she dreamed even bigger!

After high school, Regina went to West Texas A&M University, where she earned a Bachelor of Science degree in mass communications. She has worked as the news producer for KVVI, which is the ABC affiliate, ProNews 7 television station, in Amarillo, Texas. While working there she was honored by the Texas Governor's Committee on People with Disabilities with the 2003 Barbara Jordan Media Award. She has received other honors as well, including being crowned 2003 Miss Wheelchair Texas.

Today Regina serves as the executive director for the Texas State Independent Living Council. "I want to take independent living to a whole new level," Regina says confidently. And who would dare try to stand in her way?

She has been dropped by airline personnel while being transferred from her wheelchair to the airline seat. She has been on food stamps, has gone through poverty, been in three wrecks, and was slammed into a car when a friend pushing her in her wheelchair let go on a hill. And though the boy who shot Regina has full use of his arms and legs, she feels her life has turned out even better than his.

Today Regina is living her dreams because when she was a child…she refused to quit!

"Only those willing to risk going too far will discover how far it is possible to go."

– Miles Hilton-Barber

www.MilesHilton-Barber.com

6
Challenge the Naysayers
Miguel Aguayo

"I was born and raised in Chicago, Illinois, and came into the world in 1955," Miguel says. "I'm the second child of four siblings with three boys and one girl. I have an older brother and a younger one. My sister was the baby of the family. In my early years, we played a lot of baseball and football. However, I gravitated to music and guitar playing – something that I had a talent for."

Miguel's parents gave their musically-talented son a guitar for his seventh birthday. He could spend hours on end strumming, fingering chords, plucking out the melodies of familiar songs, and always trying to emulate his favorite artists – The Beatles, The Rolling Stones, and The Doors. Yes, from a very young age, Miguel knew that music was his passion. Miguel remembers, "A lot of my free time was spent strumming and setting up garage bands."

By the age of thirteen, Miguel and a couple of his friends had formed a garage band. He played six-string guitar, with another guy on bass guitar and a third band member on drums. This trio practiced every chance they got, with the goal of one day playing gigs for whom they believed would be their adoring fans.

Miguel began to pick up other instruments. He learned to play the saxophone, the French horn, and the trumpet. In fact, by his freshman year in high school, he tried out and was accepted into the concert band as second trumpeter. There was no doubt –

Miguel loved music. But what would happen if this love, this passion was taken away from him?

Miguel remembers when it all began to change. "In March 1970, during my freshman year of high school, I became ill with meningitis. I was fourteen years old. The illness started as uncontrollable chills during band practice that continued to a loss of equilibrium. This made me look like I was drunk while walking when I left school.

"I managed to make it home, where I collapsed into delirious sleep, accompanied by a deep fever. At one point, I woke without hearing, just to lapse back into a feverish sleep. At another point, I was not able to sit up. Later, my eyesight started fading as everything was blurred and my eyes were crossed to an extreme. This was when my parents took me to the hospital. I wasn't supposed to have survived. My room was in the hospice ward, filled with elderly patients who had terminal illnesses."

But, to the surprise of his doctor and nurses, Miguel made it through the first twenty-four hours and he was moved to an isolation room and received the necessary care. Miguel said, "Guess no one could figure out how to tell a newly deafened-blinded kid to croak on cue."

Miguel's only thoughts were to get better, reunite with his band, and see a girl that he had just started dating. In reflection, Miguel said, "Maybe it was denial but my optimism remained intact even after the doctors told me that it was unlikely that my hearing would return."

Miguel's recovery was slow. His eyesight came back in a few weeks. However, re-learning how to balance and walk correctly took some time. The hospital provided a lip-reading therapist who tried to encourage Miguel to focus on communicating through the oralist method. American Sign Language (ASL)

was never suggested to him. After about four months, Miguel was discharged from the hospital.

Miguel always liked school and did well. "But," he said, "my grades deteriorated in high school as my hearing declined. I had to graduate from summer school." Despite the many frustrations Miguel experienced by being the only student at his school who was deaf, he did not drop out. "That wasn't in the picture," he said.

Adjusting to deafness was a challenge. Miguel said, "Denial is a funny thing. It makes deafened people avoid facing facts; it delays getting the help that is needed to cope with life as a deafened person. However, in my case, it softened the blow by giving me time to come to acceptance my life was changed permanently."

While becoming deaf was not an experience he welcomed, Miguel never raged against it or became overly despondent. "I didn't view myself as being less a person even as my hearing made its final collapse into lifelong silence. The painful aspect was how my deafness changed other people and how quickly I was reduced to second class citizenry. I lost friends at school. My girlfriend made it clear that she wanted to date someone who could hear and broke up with me. I became isolated in a room of family members as attempts to strike up conversations with me were few. When family members tried to converse with me, the interactions were short engagements."

Socially, there was no single event that Miguel believes was particularly painful, save for going to a party just to watch everyone talking, laughing and having a good time. "Interacting with me was too much an inconvenience for them," he said. "It was even more frustrating when some individuals made perfunctory attempts to communicate, only to give up."

Eventually, Miguel started picking up finger spelling and some rudimentary sign language so he could start socializing with people of deaf culture. As his signing skills became more fluent, his integration within the deaf community became more established, even though he, as a deafened person, did not have the same experiences as people who were born deaf. The common ground that Miguel shared with deaf culture was related to living in an inaccessible, auditory-based society. But what about his passion – his music?

Miguel said, "I tried to hold on to that dream as long as I could. A short-term recovery of hearing in one ear made it easy to deny the inevitable. After a few years, reality caught up with me and I had no recourse but to sell my guitar – despite how painful it was doing so."

Losing this dream, however, did not strip Miguel of another one. That dream was to earn a degree from a university. "I always felt that college was in my future," Miguel said. "However, my parents encouraged me to get a job after graduating high school instead. Compounding this, my high school counselor was a lot more direct. He said that deaf people do not have a chance in college and my only recourse was to find factory work or be at risk of becoming a welfare recipient."

So with just a high school diploma, Miguel embarked on a career path that led to an interesting collection of jobs, but without any real connection to or opportunities for advancing a career. He found work as mail clerk, a messenger, a political campaign gofer, a landscaping crew member, a butcher's assistant, a short order cook, a plastic extrusion die operator, a shipping clerk, a pizza maker, a machine shop operator, and then as a machinist set-up man.

"The discrimination that I experienced looking for work angered me. Many job interviews became untracked once the hiring manager realized I was deaf. The irony of it all was that

the managers I worked for thought highly of my work. One even confessed that she tried out seven other guys in the messenger role before giving me a chance because she was unsure how a deaf guy could navigate the streets of Chicago's loop – as if deaf people always stay home trembling in fear – only to discover that I was the best candidate of the group that she interviewed."

Would employers and counselors see the best in Miguel? Could they look past the hearing loss and listen to what he wanted for his life? What he wanted was to go to college and earn a degree. Miguel said, "I once came close to giving up on life. At that point, I had spent most of my career moving from one dead-end job to another, only to finally have a vocational career counselor land employment for me with the U. S. Postal Service." The U.S. Postal Service is a great employer. However, this was not what Miguel wanted out of life.

"I had always felt that it was my destiny to earn a university degree," he said, "and it did not look like that would ever happen once my fifth year anniversary as a mail handler had passed."

What helped Miguel find his path was meeting other deafened people. He attests that his single, most memorable experience during this period was attending a party hosted by the Association of Late-Deafened Adults (ALDA).

He said, "This was the first time that I had encountered so many deafened people. People coming from all walks of life. Many did not sign as fluently as I could. In fact, those that knew some sign language used much more rudimental signing. I was able to share my life experience with them and feel a genuine understanding. Moreover, I had empathy for their experiences, even those who had a rougher time coping with deafness."

"After this party," Miguel continued, "I started getting involved by attending the new ALDA self-help meetings and, shortly afterwards, became a group leader." Experiencing the deaf culture, serving in leadership roles in ALDA, and now with ten years' experience working for the U.S. Postal Service, Miguel was ready to charge toward a dream he had carried with him since his youth. That dream was to earn a university degree, something no one in his immediate or extended family had ever done.

In 1993, Miguel left his hometown of Chicago, Illinois, and enrolled in the social work program at the Rochester Institute of Technology in Rochester, New York. It was there that his dream came true. He earned his first college degree, a Bachelor of Science degree in social work. Miguel said, "After graduating from the program with a BSSW degree, I moved to Waterloo in Ontario, Canada, for a Master of Social Work degree from Wilfrid Laurier University."

During post-secondary education, Miguel Aguayo received the Outstanding Baccalaureate Student Award, was inducted into the Alpha Sigma Lambda Society and the Nathaniel Rochester Society, and received the Kearse Writing Award. In addition, he was on the dean's list for ten consecutive quarters. All of this was achieved by a young man who was not expected to even go to college.

Mr. Aguayo continues, "In hindsight, I believe that I should not have allowed myself to be influenced by the advice of others with regards to what I could or could not do. Had I sought out information and asked questions, I would have learned that two deaf-friendly colleges existed [Gallaudet University and Rochester Institute of Technology/National Technical Institute for the Deaf] and I would have enrolled much earlier than I did."

When asked what he believes was the main key to his success, Mr. Aguayo is quick to say, "Having role models of other deafened people who have been successful, and being strong enough to finally face my challenges head on." He also admits that it was necessary for him to make sacrifices along the way. He said, "I spent five years working full-time on the graveyard shift at the Rochester postal facility while attending full-time classes at college, just to graduate debt-free. Graduating with a grade point average of B+ overall and a perfect A in my principle field of study was the icing on the cake!"

One of his former employers, the Canadian Imperial Bank of Commerce, received no less than six awards for diversity recruitment for a program that Mr. Aguayo developed and managed.

In addition, this organization honored him with its prestigious Human Resources Circle of Excellence Award.

Today Mr. Aguayo describes his most meaningful and valuable job, in which he now is helping others to live their dreams. He said, "I am currently managing a unit within the Ontario Disability Support Program called the Employer Outreach Secretariat. Our mandate is to create increased employment opportunities for people with disabilities by consulting with employers, identifying real and perceived barriers to hiring job seekers from this population, and finding solutions that work. I manage a small staff that does research, designing of tools, and engaging in projects that communicate to employers the best practices for recruiting, hiring and retention."

Mr. Aguayo advises, "It's OK to dream, but don't get caught up being a daydreamer. Create a life and career plan based on solid and complete information, not on other peoples' perception of your capacity. Set your goals based on what is in your heart, ask questions, challenge the naysayers, set your sights, damn the torpedoes, and go full speed ahead."

"When I was in my early years (first through fifth grade), learning disabilities were an unknown entity. Those of us that had these problems were simply viewed as unintelligent, and from my perspective the greatest sadness was that we viewed ourselves the same way."

– Fred Epstein, M.D., world-famous pioneer in brain stem and spinal cord surgery, and co-author of
If I Get to Five: What Children Can Teach Us About Courage and Character.

7
I Followed My Own Plan, Not Theirs
Sarah Stup

"With no voice but many thoughts, I was part animal and part human in their school," Sarah recalls. "A school for rejects. A school for mostly silent souls inside broken bodies." Sarah wanted to go to her sister's school. Her sister, three years older, attended a so-called "normal school."

But Sarah was different.

Her mother, Judy, explains, "Naturally, the schools Sarah entered were wary about their ability to serve Sarah, as were we."

"There were no words or actions coming from my busy body to prove that a real girl was inside," Sarah recounts. "My body did what it pleased and hardly ever listened to my instructions. Instead it darted about, squealed, and angered everyone. It repeated actions and could not stop. It jumped from high places and ate dirt. No one heard its silent words that said, 'I am smart.'"

Sarah was born in the small town of Frederick, Maryland, less than fifty miles northwest of our nation's capital. It was a short drive west from Baltimore, the largest city in Maryland, whose motto is, "The greatest city in America." The year was 1983 when Sarah said hello to this world.

Nothing out of the ordinary presented itself during Sarah's first three years. Her world, like that of other young children, was filled with wonder, playing, observing, questioning, imitating, and actively exploring everything around her.

"Sarah was quite healthy at birth," Sarah's mother said. "She developed normally until she was about two-and-a half or three years old. She communicated in short sentences and could identify her letters and numbers quite early.

"She became increasingly active, climbing and running about, and was more impulsive," Sarah's mother continues. "Then, at about three years of age, a time when communication accelerates quickly for most children, Sarah's abilities stayed the same and then later her language became more regimented. Obsessive activities began, such as coloring with a crayon, touching the point to her forehead, and then lining up the crayons perfectly, only to begin again.

"Sarah received diagnoses of attention deficit hyperactive disorder (ADHD), and communication impaired, almost immediately, but it was years before doctors gave the actual diagnosis of autism. In those days, there was reluctance to diagnose a child with autism, likely because the prognosis for the future was so very poor."

Autism is a spectrum disorder, meaning its symptoms vary from person to person. Sarah's disability is considered significant. She does not speak and has limited motor skills.

"Sarah never acquired speech beyond a few words," Sarah's mother describes, "and rarely for communication purposes. But, at age eight, she began pointing at a piece of paper with letters and spelling out words for her speech therapist at school. Suddenly she could share her feelings and preferences with us. Repeatedly, she typed out 'I smart.' It was so important to her to have us realize she was always inside. Still, it is surprising how she was still the same person and how well we knew her even before she could communicate on that new level."

"When I was a child," Sarah says, "music listening, book reading, and swinging were fun for me. Voices of people hurt my ears. Park visiting was a favorite then and now. Nature is my connection, not friends who come and go. God and family are my loves.

"I loved learning about our world and planning ways to be a good citizen, but because I had no sounding voice I felt lonely and scared. School expected me to hide my disability and be a fake normal. Autism is part of who I am.

"My all time favorite subjects were math and history, and my least favorite was health.

"My greatest challenge as a child was being weird with autism. Autism was awful, so people thought I was strange and naughty. Actually I was a polite person inside a body that did as it pleased and never listened to me. Kids staring hurt my feelings as well as adults complaining.

"I felt like I was smart inside a dumb body. I was wishful, scared, silent, and hopeful."

One of Sarah's wishes and hopes had always been to attend regular school. She had been attending a school for children who had a variety of disabilities. In describing this school, Sarah said, "It was a place of fear and music and tears and snacks. It was a place decorated with normality, but dozens and dozens of school buses rounded up imperfection and corralled it there."

But then something happened. Something that would change everything. Something that would not only have an impact on Sarah's life but also on the lives of everyone who would come to know Sarah. She began to communicate. Oh, not in the traditional way that most communicate. She still did not speak.

But Sarah learned that she could have her voice be heard through writing.

She was eight years old when she began to learn to type and, for the first time, through typing, Sarah's voice was finally being heard.

There was someone inside – a child not really that different from other children. She was a child with likes and dislikes, a child with hopes as well as fears, a child who wanted to be heard. And the message that everyone heard loud and clear was that Sarah wanted to go to regular school. And so, at age eight, Sarah entered fourth grade at a regular school.

Was it easy? No. Sarah did not fit the mold. She was different. She communicated in a very unique way and this made many people uneasy and just not sure how to react. "Of course," Sarah's mother recalls, "there were teachers and students who were strong advocates and friends to Sarah, especially when she was very young."

However, Sarah remembers, "A time passed when some school staff would not allow me to practice or take high school assessments to graduate. They thought my helper should not be talking or directing my eyes to my keyboard or the test materials.

"When I was banned from these test activities I felt unworthy and sad. I wished to prove my competence, but I had no control. I wished to be a good student, but a wall of doubt kept me separate. I wished to be free of the fear of differences.

"Many times I saw myself as they did. There was a time in high school when I played 'dumb' because it seemed to me that some school staff in one school I attended were troubled by my being intelligent. I decided they would be happier if they educated only poor thinkers. It made me sad to let them think they were right, but I was very tired of their doubting me. I wished to give up because I needed peace."

Thoughts of giving up did creep into Sarah's mind. These pilfering thoughts creep into everyone's mind, especially when others are saying you don't belong. It's what you do with those limiting thoughts that will determine how you will live the rest of your life.

This young teenaged girl found the will to press on, even though most of the people around her did not understand her.

Sarah said, "Hope troops along through stop signs. New paths can be carved out. A step can be climbed. Wishes are important beginnings. One day I rode away from their doubts and climbed the stairs of my own hopes and wishes. I followed my own plan, not theirs."

Sarah had discovered a major key to success: to follow your own plan, not someone else's. Next, she focused on her passion.

"I hoped to become a writer so that I could let others know that those with disabilities and other differences are real people who are worth lots," Sarah said.

Ultimately, Sarah was allowed to take the high school assessment exams for graduation and, in 2004, Sarah, at age twenty, graduated from high school with honors.

"Aaron Stephens of The Arc of Frederick County helped me get the skills and help I needed to become a published author," Sarah said. "When boxes of books arrived with my words in print, I knew my characters would march out to let kids know we people with autism are not empty shells with no inhabitants.

"Sometimes I get shy and scared about being an author, but writing is my only voice. It is who I am and what I need. When the world heard my silent typing voice I became a real person. With writing I am alive. When I write I am not held back at all. I can be anyone or anything, and I can go new places with new ideas. For me, writing is power and freedom. Writing is what I need.

"A place I love to write is my cozy kitchen booth. I know its sights and sounds well, so autism can rest there. Time spent typing and planning and dreaming pleases me. Paper strips hold my words that reach out to you from my world of silence and loneliness.

"My wish to help people with developmental disabilities get better lives is what I am seeking with my words. I like to send messages of hope and understanding from the real people who are inside bodies that work differently. The words can change minds.

"Those of us with disabilities and other differences are real people inside bodies that work differently. We are worth knowing.

"Robert Frost's poetry makes me see new in the ordinary, and Anne Shirley in Anne of Green Gables makes me laugh inside. Anne Frank and I both write about hiding.

"When the reader joins me inside my character's view of the world, the reader listens in a new way. Views must entertain to be contemplated long. Entertainment is a key that unlocks and opens minds and hearts. Entertainment may be less important, but it is first."

A child who could not communicate in the traditional way grows up to teach others how to best communicate with a person who has autism or another developmental disability.

"Find ways to help others to become good citizens and God's tools," Sarah says. "Ask for the help you need to fulfill your own dreams. Carve new pathways. Find ways to make the world a better place for those with disabilities and other differences."

Excerpts taken, with permission, from *Are Your Eyes Listening?* and from Ms. Stup's essay, "Teacher's Pet," found at her website, www.SarahStup.com/sarahs_essays.htm .

Today Ms. Stup is an acclaimed author and an advocate for people with disabilities. Her books include, *Do-Si-Do with Autism*, a book for children about Taylor the Turtle who has autism, and, *Are Your Eyes Listening? Collected Works for Adults: Reflections on Autism, Life and Love.*

Ms. Stup is also the recipient of awards including the 2004 Arc of Maryland Self-Advocate of the Year Award and the 2004 Frances and Lease Bussard Award for Self-Advocacy.

To learn more about Sarah Stup or to order her books, visit www.SarahStup.com.

"People shouldn't let physical disabilities limit their ambitions. You can't afford to be disabled in spirit as well as physically. People won't have time for you."

– Professor Stephen W. Hawking

www.hawking.org.uk

8
I Could Become a Voice
Tony Volpentest

"I'll race you to that tree," Tony's classmate challenged him.

"You're on," Tony challenged back. And the two boys were off.

And the winner is…the other boy.

"Okay," Tony thought to himself, "but one day I'm going to be the fastest runner in the world."

There's nothing wrong with dreaming big dreams. But there was just one tiny problem with Tony's dream: he has no feet…and no hands. How could a child who was born with no feet or hands even think that he could grow up to be the fastest runner in the world? That would be impossible…or would it?

"Ever since I was young," Tony said, "I have believed that if you can dream it, you can achieve it.

"When I was fifteen years old, I joined my high school's track team," Tony said. "I knew no one got cut from that team and I figured it would be a way to make new friends."

But in every race, whether racing against teammates during practice or against runners from an opposing team, Tony always came in last, every single time. Why not give up? No one would fault a teenager who loses every race for quitting the track team – especially if that teenager has no feet.

But Tony wasn't thinking of quitting. He was focused on finding a solution that would help him run faster.

It was during his junior year in high school that a solution surfaced. That was when Tony was first introduced to Flex-Feet, prosthetic feet that allow the person to walk or run more naturally and farther with less fatigue and discomfort. This new pair of feet was the answer he had been searching for. Now, in his senior year of high school, this last-place runner was finishing second and third place consistently and, best of all, he lettered, something just a couple of years earlier would have been impossible.

"I knew," Tony said, "if I concentrated and visualized myself running, I could break those world records. I could start changing stereotypes people have of people with disabilities. I could make a difference, I could become a voice."

Changing stereotypes is exactly what he did. Once stared at for having no feet, now millions were staring in disbelief at this young man who was making running history. In 1990, at age seventeen, Tony took home three gold medals at the world championships in St. Etienne, France. From last place to gold medals! Unbelievable! But Tony was just getting started.

In 1992, he set two world records at the Barcelona Paralympic Games, while also claiming two gold medals in the 100 and 200 meter races, and silver in the 400 meter relay.

No time to look back. No time to focus on his disability. Tony focused on where he wanted to go. And he was going there faster than anyone else.

At the Atlanta, Georgia, Paralympic Games in July of 1996, Tony not only took the gold medal but also set another world record in the 100 meter dash, running it in 11.36 seconds. Next, he took another gold medal in the 200 meter dash.

Then in 1999, at the International Sport Organization for the Disabled (ISOD) World Championships in Barcelona, Spain, Tony claimed still more gold medals for both the 100 and the 200 meter races. He set still another new world record in the 200 meter, crossing the finish line in 22.85 seconds.

Altogether, Tony has won 22 gold medals, 4 silver, and 1 bronze. How different his life would have turned out if he had quit back in high school when he was losing every race. But Tony Volpentest refused to quit. Thus, a champion was born!

He has won numerous honors and awards including the International Olympic Committee President's Disabled Athletes Award, the United States Olympic Committee Athlete of the Year Award, and the Franklin Delano Roosevelt Award for the Physically Challenged, and has served as the national spokesman for Shriners Hospitals, just to name a few.

Today Tony is a highly sought-after motivational speaker. He has become a voice, a symbol of what is possible when you refuse to quit.

Who could have ever guessed that the child born with no feet or hands would one day grow up to become an international sports hero in track. Tony is living proof that it is often the child who is the least likely to succeed who actually grows up to achieve more than most ever believe to be possible!

Tony says, "The human spirit knows no limits, regardless of the physical being. It can overcome any obstacle and inspires greatness in all aspects of life. My mission is to show just how brightly the human spirit can shine!"

For more information about Tony Volpentest, please visit www.TonyVolpentest.com.

"I have enjoyed a wonderful career of writing books for children. Who could have guessed that little girl that was having such a tough time in school would end up an illustrator and author."

– Patricia Polacco, award-winning author who did not learn to read until she was nearly fourteen years old, which was when she was finally diagnosed as having a learning disability known as dyslexia.

www.PatriciaPolacco.com

9
They Make Us Prevail
Laurel Marshall

"Take her home and enjoy her...she will not live past the age of two." This was the paralyzing announcement from the doctor to my devastated parents. Although they knew something was wrong, even the best doctors were perplexed. The diagnosis, as well as the time left for me, a tiny blonde toddler, remained a mystery.

As horrific as this news was, my parents never let on. They took one day at a time. The doctors were obviously wrong – I am still here! But, it took quite a while to get the semi-confirmed diagnosis of muscular dystrophy.

Long before this diagnosis, my parents together had made a personal decision to hold me to high standards and hold me accountable for my actions. They always made me feel normal. They taught me that there was nothing that I could not do. More importantly, I believed it.

All my life, I have been told by both friends and strangers that I am an inspiration to them. "Who, me?" I would think. It was hard for me to understand in my younger years. In fact, it was almost embarrassing. I was just like anyone else. In reality, I was not.

Muscular dystrophy made walking difficult. In the seventh grade, I had to get crutches and braces for my legs in order to walk. In the eighth grade, I fell and broke my hip, placing me in a wheelchair for good. My muscle weakness has not only affected my legs, it also affected my hands, leaving them with an inability to grasp. To me

as a child though, I was still like everyone else. I was determined not to stand out and I found a way to do what everyone else was doing, even if I had to do it in an unconventional way.

For example, when I lost the ability to write with my one hand, I found a way to write with two hands. I vividly remember that day in the eighth grade. As I was taking notes during Mrs. Young's lecture, my index finger would not wrap around my pen. It was extremely frustrating, causing me to fall behind in the note taking. After several unsuccessful tries of wrapping my finger around that darn pen, I quickly had to figure out a new way. After all, I was falling behind. Within those few short minutes, I lost the ability to write with one hand, but instantaneously discovered a way to write with two. There was no other option. No discussion with parents or doctors. Was it perseverance or survival? Maybe a little of both. I just did it – I had to do it.

After eighth grade graduation, all my friends were going to attend Ursuline Academy, an all-girls high school in Dallas. In my mind, that was no big deal. But my parents had serious reservations, as I would be the first student with a disability to attend this prestigious but non-accessible school. This was well before the requirements of the Americans with Disabilities Act. As nervous as they were, my parents encouraged me and never told me that I could not accomplish my goals.

I was accepted at Ursuline Academy of Dallas and I did excel. However, it was not easy being the only student at my school who used a wheelchair. It was the early 1980s, years before architectural barriers would begin to be removed. But I always had good friends who were happy to help if I needed them.

I had a good friend. To get to our physics class, she had to push me almost around the entire school to get to the only accessible entrance to the science building. To free up her hands so she could push me, we would stack her books on top of my books on my lap. I had books stacked all the way up to my chin.

Because we didn't have much time to get to class, she was almost always running as she was pushing me. Once, we were moving pretty fast down the hill toward the building when my friend lost control and we had a wipe out. I ended up on the ground with the books all around me. I remember those spills and thrills more than I remember the academic days.

During my senior year, to meet my school's requirement of community service hours, I volunteered at the Texas Scottish Rite Hospital for Children in Dallas. I wanted to give back to that hospital because I had spent a great deal of time there as a young patient. I volunteered in the schoolroom, and was the assistant to the certified teacher who taught all the hospitalized kids so that they could keep their studies up.

I fondly remember a bright-eyed, seven-year-old named Billy Bob. He had surgery on his foot, which was improving every day. His daily visits to the schoolroom helped him continue his studies. What a shock when he hobbled into the schoolroom one day with a cast on his right arm. In disbelief, I blurted out, "Billy Bob, what happened?" As we proceeded to open his first grade math book, he explained in detail how he had fallen and broken his arm as the doctors were watching his final descent down the hallway before he was to be released. As badly as I felt for him, I knew that we had to continue his studies. But he insisted that he could not write.

As I was trying to figure out how to handle the situation, I noticed a seam in his cast. Busted! He finally confessed with a grin that it was fake. He begged me not to tell the teacher because he did not want to do his schoolwork. After a laugh together, with my help, he managed to complete the assignment.

My first taste of teaching was delicious. Little did I know that this was the beginning of something very important in my life – my career as a teacher. After high school, I was ready to pursue this career.

I arrived at Texas A&M University in College Station, about three hours south of Dallas. For the first time in my life, upon arriving there, I met others who travelled by wheelchair as I did.

Texas A&M's Fish Camp is not just a place to learn Aggie jokes! It's a three-day freshman orientation camp in Palestine, Texas, that allows new students to learn Aggie traditions, start new friendships, and gain the self-confidence needed to handle and succeed in college life. This atmosphere made me feel so comfortable that I kicked off the confining leg braces I had worn since I was a child – I no longer felt the need to disguise my bird-like legs which were atrophied due to muscular dystrophy.

The acceptance I felt from the counselors and other campers touched my heart and confirmed for me that no one cared what my legs looked like. My desire to share similar experiences and help incoming students feel this type of acceptance led me to become a Fish Camp counselor, a role that I enjoyed for the next three years.

My wonderful college days were nearing an end. Though I was sad to say good-bye to everyone, I knew I had made friendships that would last a lifetime. Armed with my Bachelor of Science degree in education, I went in pursuit of a teaching job.

In 1990, I was hired to teach in the Richardson Independent School District. I certainly don't fit the stereotypical image of a teacher, and I had to overcome many obstacles in order to become one. Luckily, I believed in myself and surrounded myself with others who believed in me.

When I first started teaching at Dartmouth, I was full of self-confidence, and a bit of naivety. The principal saw potential in me and hired me. Peggy, a former teammate, now retired, told me that even though I was a successful student teacher, she initially thought there was no way I could manage a full classroom on my own. She was not alone – I later found out that this was a majority opinion among my new teaching colleagues at Dartmouth. Fortunately, I never caught on and I proved them wrong. Nearly two decades later, Peggy and I now laugh about it as she marvels at my success and longevity in teaching.

In the summer of 1997, Canine Companions for Independence invited me to attend team training in Oceanside, California, where I received my first service dog, Temecula. When I returned to Richardson, I was not prepared for the surprise reception that we would receive at Dartmouth Elementary, during summer break. Around fifty people from the surrounding neighborhood gathered in excitement to see my new arrival, just like a baby.

Every child can be successful in school. I truly believe that to the core of my being. As a teacher, I play a pivotal role in that success. At the beginning of every year, I greet the new fourth graders with a welcoming smile as they anxiously enter the classroom for the first time. Bright, cheery walls and stuffed animals from my childhood create a secure and happy environment. The feeling of warmth reassures them that this will be a comfortable place to spend this important year.

Due to my disability, the kids take actively responsible roles in the classroom. They act as my hands and feet, without judgment. From picking up a dropped chalk holder, setting up the overhead projector, or racing to grab my key so that they can be the first person to lock my purse away in my closet, they are happy to help. This demonstrates the natural giving spirit of children. I never take these acts of kindness for granted, always making the time to tell my students that I appreciate them.

"I want to be in your class, Ms. Marshall!" are the words I commonly hear from younger kids at Dartmouth. Some have older siblings, so they are eager to assist me in the classroom, like their predecessors. Most of them just want to be in a classroom with a dog. My assistance service dog, Sunny, brings awareness to the children and adults at Dartmouth of the proper etiquette when encountering a handler with a working service dog. She also brings love, warmth, and serenity just by her presence.

At the beginning of each year, I hold a demonstration for the fourth graders. During these demonstration sessions, the students learn that Sunny is a working dog, not a pet. Her job is to listen to me. They learn not to pet a working dog because that distracts them, preventing them from performing their job. They also learn about the different types of working dogs and that if a dog wears a vest in public, it is best not to disturb it.

I then put Sunny through her paces, showing off her ability to follow commands. Sunny then demonstrates her ability to pick up dropped items, retrieve the mail, get the remote, and take laundry out of the clothes dryer. Invariably, the eyes of the students light up with excitement as they teeter on the edges of their seats – giggles, as well as "oohs" and "aahs," fill the air. But more importantly, they understand through this real life demonstration that she is a special dog, providing me with important assistance to live my life each day.

Patience is a hard lesson for a child to learn. In my classroom, patience is not an option. I have a certain methodology by which I balance an overhead marker in my fingers, as my hands are unable to grip – the students watch me, almost in reverence. They patiently wait as I re-Velcro my chalk holder to my hand as I continue to teach a lesson on the blackboard. Even though it would be easy for frustration to take over, they watch me stay calm and get the mission accomplished. And, in turn, the children learn to exercise their own patience in their individual daily life challenges.

I experienced my greatest reward in teaching this past year. At first, I did not understand it. I was almost annoyed. Since I began teaching in 1990, on the second day of school, I gather all of the fourth graders in one room. I instruct them to write on a piece of paper three questions that they would like to ask me. I also tell them that they do not have to include the most obvious question – "Why are you in a wheelchair?" – as I will cover that at the beginning of the discussion. My purpose in doing this is so that little Bobby or Sue will not drift off in math class wondering why my feet do not work.

In years past, the first question is along the lines of, "What is your favorite color?" The next, something like, "What is your favorite pet?" I dutifully answer these important questions. Then, I discuss muscular dystrophy, what it is, and how it affects my muscles and my body. This usually sparks many questions not written on their papers –"How do you drive?" "How do you do your grocery shopping?" "How do you get into bed?" The questions seem endless, but it is important that I answer every one.

This year, I was confused. I went through the usual routine. After explaining muscular dystrophy, I asked if there were any other questions. Only three kids had questions. The attitude of the students appeared to be nonchalant. Never before had I seen this demeanor from my students. Later that week, after much reflection, I had an epiphany. In their eyes, having a teacher in a wheelchair with a service dog was "no big deal." What for years had been an anomaly – something strange and unique – was now the norm. I was a teacher just like any other teacher. Unknowingly, I had achieved one of my main goals as a teacher. The lesson had been learned.

When all is said and done, I want my students to carry the life lessons that they learned in fourth grade throughout their lives. When they face an obstacle, I want them to think of me. I want them to say to themselves, if Ms. Marshall can do it, so can I!

As a child, I tried to fight my imperfections. As I matured, I realized that my differences are what make me unique. They have caused me to excel. My differences have caused me to want to make a difference in the lives of my students and others.

I felt so honored when my colleagues bestowed on me the prestigious distinction of being named as the 2005-2006 Elementary Teacher of the Year for the Richardson School District.

I felt just as honored upon receiving other accolades, including being invited by the Muscular Dystrophy Association to be their honorary chairperson for their annual "Cruisin' to a Cure" benefit. This led me to serve as a devoted committee member for this event for the next four years, helping to raise tens of thousands of dollars for the Muscular Dystrophy Association (MDA).

Since MDA had given me so much support over the years, providing me with crutches, wheelchairs, and medical equipment, my involvement was just a small way of saying "Thank you."

I also attended MDA Summer Camp as a motivational speaker and dance instructor from 2000 through 2002. In this role, I spoke to teenagers with disabilities about life, college, and their favorite topic – dating! I tried to convey to them simple but important messages:

Believe in yourself, set goals, and keep a positive attitude to achieve them.

Acceptance at all levels is a basic human need. Despite differences, everyone has worth, dignity, and value. Differences are to be celebrated, not feared. Every child has value. Once a child feels, truly feels, that he is valued, that child can begin to see the value in others, even though they may be different. The child then becomes open to the differences around him, learning and growing from them instead of feeling threatened by them. The child, in time, learns that it is our differences that not only make us special, but that make us prevail.

"Passion is the great slayer of adversity. Focus on strengths and what you enjoy."

– Charles Schwab

www.schwab.com

10
From the Mundane to the Extraordinary
Geerat Vermeij, Ph.D.

"I'm going to be a conchologist when I grow up," nine-year-old Gary announced to his classmates at school.

"What in the world is that?" everyone asked.

"I'm not exactly sure," answered Gary, "but books tell me it's someone who collects and studies shells. I want to know things like: why are shells found in cold water different from those found in warm water?" he would say, pondering how the riblets of a shell felt when he moved his hands over them.

Geerat Vermeij, who adopted the American nickname Gary, was born in September of 1946 in a small Dutch town in the Netherlands, located in western Europe. He was born with a rare childhood form of glaucoma after his mother had contracted German measles while she was pregnant with him. Glaucoma is an eye disease in which there is an increased pressure in the eye. This pressure causes permanent damage to the delicate fibers in the optic nerve, which are used to transmit images from the eye to the brain.

Gary spent much of the first three and a half years of his life in hospitals as doctors attempted to relieve the constant pain and prevent further damage to the optic nerves. Despite an exhausting schedule of operations twice a week, along with all the medications,

the risk of this glaucoma causing something more serious than vision loss was increasing. It threatened to
lead to brain damage.

Doctors recommended that Gary have both of his eyes removed. This would give Gary a welcomed relief from the pain, and artificial eyes would look normal, unlike Gary's own eyes which were swollen most of the time. The final operation to remove Gary's eyes took place three months before his fourth birthday.

Gary said, "My world was not black and hopeless. It sparkled as it did before, but now with sounds, odors, shapes, and textures." A few weeks after the operation, he traveled with his family to another town to be fitted for his first pair of prosthetic eyes. He would have blue eyes as his own had been.

"The loss of vision does not rob the blind of their ability to learn about the world," Gary said. "My parents missed no opportunity to treat me as a fully capable and responsible member of the family."

Gary began attending a school for the blind just weeks before he turned four years old. The education he received was excellent, but he was totally segregated from the sighted world. Gary's parents knew that in order for their youngest son to be able to make it in the sighted world during his adult years, he would have to be a part of it during his childhood.

When Gary was eight, they made the decision to leave their Dutch homeland and move the family to the United States. Gary celebrated his ninth birthday on the North Atlantic Ocean as they sailed for the U.S. in September of 1955. They arrived in Dover, New Jersey, later that month.

As he began third grade in public school, Gary remembers, "I felt powerless and overwhelmed as I tried to learn to speak and understand English and to be understood." He was also the only student in his school who was blind.

His parents took an active role in teaching Gary many things. Gary's dad introduced him to his outdoor surroundings and to studying plants. "My dad would read the World Atlas to me as I labeled maps with Braille," Gary recounts. "I read everything I could get my hands on, including the seven-volume Braille dictionary in my classroom."

It was his fourth grade teacher who first kindled his scientific curiosity. Gary said, "Mrs. Colberg brought to school shells she had collected from Florida. These shells felt as if they had been crafted by a sculptor with an eye for regularity and intricate detail. My fourth grade teacher had not only given my hands an unforgettable aesthetic treat, but she aroused in me a lasting curiosity about things unknown."

Gary continued to seek out books on shells but none of these books satisfied his curiosity. He contacted the American Museum of Natural History, asking if someone there could help him identify a few shells. "Yes," was the response he got, along with an invitation to come to the museum.

In the spring of 1961, now fourteen years old, Gary traveled with his mother and older brother to New York City for his first visit with professional malacologists, people who make their living studying shells and the animals who build them. Recognizing Gary's passion for this science, the malacologist counseled him to consider studying biology, specifically the area of fossils.

It was recommended to Gary that he subscribe to malacological journals so he could read about the research currently being done. A high school teenager reading malacological journals? Sure, why not?! Since they were not available in Braille, Gary's mother gladly read every article in the journals to her teenaged son.

"Science seemed to come alive in these articles," Gary said, "unlike the dry facts and laws found in school science textbooks. I also learned that scientists sometimes made mistakes and, at times, their conclusions were incomplete. This gave me hope that one day I might be able to contribute original research. I began to believe, without a doubt, that science was approachable for me."

As Gary entered his senior year of high school, he learned that he ranked first in his senior class. The Commission for the Blind had been providing Gary with the financial assistance to hire people to read to him. The primary purpose for this service is to help the person who is blind achieve successful employment.

Gary confidently discussed his plans with his counselor at the Commission for the Blind. "I will enroll in college with a major in biology. I know I will need to not only earn an undergraduate degree but also a Ph.D. in order to be employed as a researcher. I plan to earn all of these degrees from an Ivy League university."

His counselor quietly listened. She had counseled many high school students in the past. They all had such big dreams for their lives. But, too often, she had seen them give up in frustration when the brick walls began to appear before them.

Believing Gary was planning to embark on an unrealistic journey, she took a deep breath and then began slowly, "Gary, biology is too visually-oriented. You will never be able to find a job with a degree in biology. In addition, Gary," she continued, "your test results indicate that attaining a Ph.D. is out of your reach. You will need to study something else, not biology. And let's plan on you attending a small liberal arts college. That will be more in your reach than an Ivy League university."

Gary's heart sank. Without his counselor's approval of his plans, the Commission for the Blind could halt all financial aid. His parents could not pay for all the readers he would need in college.

He thought back to the advice he had been given at the Museum of Natural History. Why not work on fossils?

"I could still do all the biology I wanted," Gary explained. "In fact, biology lies at the core of paleontology, but on paper at least I could deemphasize those aspects of biology that rely heavily on microscopes or other visual techniques."

"That sounds like a plan that can work," Gary's counselor happily admitted. "I will approve this new plan."

Still headstrong, he applied for admission to Princeton, an Ivy League university. Not only was Gary accepted, but he was also granted a scholarship. Upon graduating from high school, he was off to Princeton. Everything seemed to be going so well for Gary. "But I was in over my head," Gary admits. "I was struggling."

As the first semester ended, Gary learned just how poor his grades were – a D in physics and a C in everything else. He had gone from being at the top of his class in high school to the bottom of his class in college.

It is times like this when the tough decisions have to be made. Give up or continue to work harder than you've ever worked before? He had come so far from losing his sight at age three and struggling to learn to speak English while in elementary school. He had not come this far to now give up.

Gary sought advice from his two advisors at Princeton who recommended that combining biology and geology would be a better plan for him. Gary agreed. He immersed himself in his studies following this new plan.

His grades turned around. He rose from the bottom of his class at Princeton to the top 5%. In 1968, Gary accomplished something most had believed would be impossible for him: he graduated from Princeton with a bachelor's degree in biology!

It was now time to begin graduate work. He was accepted to Yale University in February of 1968 with a full fellowship. While at Yale, he met Edith, another graduate biology student. Could this be the woman he had always hoped to find? Gary had always been quite shy, but he knew what he wanted. "She would have to be very smart, very interesting, and attractive to me, which meant a good feminine voice and silky clothes. Edith was perfect," Gary said. He was thrilled to learn that Edith would be one of his readers. This gave them a chance to get to know each other in a quiet and comfortable setting.

"We sighted ones can't help but look," Edith said, "and it's just a good thing I thought Gary was cute. I don't know why – it was something about him. I think his personality just came through everything, even the way he turned around. He walks fast and he swings his cane more like a weapon clearing the path.

"We talked about the blindness pretty early on. I said it was weird to me, because I loved looking at things so much. He assured me that he was a basically happy person, and that he enjoyed his take on the world as much as any human could do, and I soon realized this to be true.

"I remember being in the Caribbean that first time, and watching Gary put his hand under a rock to feel around in spite of knowing there might be really bad biting or stinging animals under there. I tried doing it, and I was thinking, 'He needs his hands a million times more than I do and I can't make myself do this.'"

Gary smiles as he injects, "These acts showed that I had real courage, something Edith found attractive."

"I don't know if it was a good or a bad reason," Edith continued, "but it helped to trigger some internal decision to keep going on this strange love affair."

Gary graduated from Yale University in 1971 with his Ph.D. in biology and geology. He was hired to teach at the University of Maryland, and so in August of 1971, Dr. Vermeij began his work there.

Best of all, he now had his wife, Edith, by his side after she had completed her Ph.D. at Yale. Their daughter was born in 1981 and today shares her parents' love for biology and nature.

Today Dr. Vermeij is considered to be one of the most accomplished evolutionary biologists and paleontologists of our time. He is the world's leading authority on ancient and living mollusks, particularly shells, and how species arm themselves and survive. Dr. Vermeij is a professor of geology at the University of California at Davis, where he has been since 1989.

"I indeed entered science through the study of shells," Dr. Vermeij says, "but a deep love of science quickly extended my interests. This deep love – indeed, my utter devotion to science – is an integral part of me, and accounts in large measure for my persistence in pursuing my goals.

"I continue to be extremely active in research and teaching," Dr. Vermeij says. "I am on the Board of Trustees of the California Academy of Sciences, and serve as editor of my third journal [*The Veliger*, a journal devoted to mollusks]."

Remembering the day his fourth grade teacher introduced him to the study of shells, he said, "On that day, a wonderful teacher set the course for one man's life. To be a scientist is one of the most fulfilling ways of living a life that I can imagine. It is a profound privilege daily to observe natural phenomena and to seek evidence-based explanations for them. The key to success in the kind of science I practice is the ability – indeed, the intense desire – to observe everything, from the mundane to the extraordinary, and to think about what one observes.

"Science is about recognizing and solving puzzles, about putting the jumble of facts into a coherent theory, about communicating this to others. I observe, I read and read and read, I think, I write, I teach. None of this is closed to the blind or to anyone else with a physical shortcoming. Keen observation, reflection, a long attention span, hard work and persistence are necessary qualities for success in science, and all are attainable by those who want them."

Excerpts taken with permission, from *Privileged Hands: A Scientific Life,* by Geerat Vermeij.

Dr. Vermeij has also authored four other books entitled, *Biogeography and Adaptation: Patterns of Marine Life*, *Evolution and Escalation: An Ecological History of Life*, *A Natural History of Shells*, and *Nature, An Economic History*.

"Courage does not always roar. Sometimes, it is the quiet voice at the end of the day saying, 'I will try again tomorrow.'"

– Anonymous

11
My Eyes Are on the Finish Line and I'm Not Stopping Until I Get There
Kelly Sutton

Kelly and her dad were building a race car that she planned to drive in a race in just a few months. Her dad, Ed Sutton, a race car driver himself, knew what was needed to make the car competitive on the track.

Ever since Kelly had been five years old, she knew when she grew up that she would be a race car driver just like her dad and granddad. When other kids were skateboarding and riding bicycles, Kelly was riding motorcycles and racing go-karts. And now, the building of her very own race car was nearing completion.

"Kelly," her mother called out to the garage, "it's time to clean up. You have school tomorrow."

"Okay, Mom," Kelly called back as she wiped some grease from her arms.

"Yes, this car will be the finest one on the track come this fall," sixteen-year-old Kelly said to herself. She smiled as she pictured herself driving it on the track in front of the cheering crowd. As Kelly walked into the house she wondered, "Why does that keep happening? The tingling and numbness in my fingers and hands – why does that keep happening?"

She had first noticed it three years earlier, when she was thirteen years old. Her parents had taken Kelly to several doctors over the past couple of years. "I've seen her go from being a very active, athletic teenaged girl," Kelly's mom described to the latest doctor, "to being very weak and tired and having no energy to do the things she loves to do, like race."

Her mom went on to describe more disturbing symptoms. "I've noticed that she loses her balance sometimes and there are also times when she just seems so sad and depressed. This just isn't my Kelly."

"Teenagers are often clumsy," the doctor assured Kelly's mom. "It's nothing to be alarmed about. And mood changes often occur during the teenage years. The depression will go away."

But these symptoms persisted, until one morning Kelly awoke to discover that she had no feeling on the entire right side of her body. The next trip to the doctor would bring forth some answers, answers that Kelly and her family never imagined.

"Kelly," the doctor spoke as he faced Kelly's parents, "has a neurological disease called multiple sclerosis." Pausing for a moment to allow his words to sink in, the doctor then continued, "We will need to do an MRI and a spinal tap on Kelly to determine which form of multiple sclerosis she has."

"My life is over," was Kelly's first thought as she sat in shock trying to make sense of the doctor's words. "I thought my world had come to an end. I didn't want anybody to know. I didn't want to go on living. I just wanted to fall into a hole and just die."

As the days passed, Kelly and her parents read everything they could find to help them better understand this disease. They learned that MS, as it is often called, is a chronic disease that affects the central nervous system, which consists of the brain, spinal cord, and optic nerves.

There is a fatty tissue called myelin which surrounds and protects the nerve fibers of the central nervous system. In MS, myelin is lost in multiple areas, leaving scar tissue called sclerosis. When the myelin is lost or destroyed, the ability of the nerves to communicate with the brain is disrupted.

The symptoms a person with MS has are determined by which nerve fibers lose their myelin protection. For this reason, the symptoms are unpredictable and vary from person to person. They can include extreme fatigue, loss of eyesight, problems with balance that make walking difficult or impossible, slurred speech, and a few others.

The MRI and spinal tap that were done on Kelly revealed that she had the most common form of multiple sclerosis, known as relapsing-remitting MS. With this type, relapses can occur at any time, after which new symptoms may appear or existing symptoms may worsen.

Kelly was next examined by an MS specialist. He did not sugar-coat his prognosis. "Kelly," he said, "you have about eight to ten years before you will lose your ability to walk."

"I was devastated," she recalls. "I was sixteen years old, and all I wanted to do was race."

Should she just give up? If her dreams were all going to be ripped away from her in a few years, was it worth it to press on? You bet it was! Kelly's passion for racing was too strong.

Give up? No way.

Kelly stopped focusing on her fears about MS and began focusing once again on racing. She spent four years racing mini stock cars locally.

Then, in 1995, less than seven years after her diagnosis of MS, Kelly's childhood dream of racing at Daytona International Speedway seemed like it was about to come true. But just one week before Kelly was to leave for Daytona to participate in her first big race, she hit a patch of ice and smashed her car into a tree.

The accident left Kelly with several injuries, including broken ribs, a collapsed lung, and a dislocated right hip and left shoulder. The injuries, however, were just the beginning. The accident also triggered a relapse of Kelly's MS.

Have you ever been so close to realizing a life-long dream that you could almost taste it, only to have it snatched away from you as you reached out to claim it?

Kelly's MS symptoms persisted until finally, with no other choice, Kelly had to move from her racecar into a wheelchair. This was exactly what the doctor had predicted several years earlier.

"I had to rely on my family for help for almost everything, including help with showering, getting into bed, and so much more, for nearly a year," she said. "No way could I have gotten in a race car."

Many might have believed that this twenty-three-year-old should just stop dreaming of one day racing professionally. Racecar drivers' bodies are under a lot of stress during a race, and they must be in peak physical and mental condition.

Not exactly sure if or how she could ever race again, Kelly was motivated to try when her dad showed up at her house with a training car without wheels.

"It looked like a go-kart with no wheels. My dad had hooked the steering wheel to two shocks which provided enough resistance to equal fifty pounds of pressure each time I turned the wheel one direction. He did the same thing to the pedals. He told me when I could do 100 laps in that, when I could turn the wheel 100 times, we were going racing again."

Knowing that diet, exercise, and medication all play a role in managing MS, Kelly worked to find the right balance of these three elements. Just finding the right medication was not an easy task.

She had to find a medication that would not do her more harm than good.

It was the medication called Copaxone, a daily injection that literally gave Kelly her life back. It got her out of the wheelchair and back in the driver's seat. And in this driver's seat, Kelly is moving 190 miles per hour.

Are there any more roadblocks jumping out in her way? Absolutely. That's part of the journey.

"It's like when we were running thirteenth in the Goody's Dash Series, in 2001. We had two laps to go and my Pontiac Sunfire conked out. I drifted into our pit and they started working on it. We finally got it fired up, and I took off. I could have just ridden into the pits, got out of my car and quit, but I didn't. I came in 21st – a great finish for my first time at Daytona."

Not only that, in 2001 Kelly made history by becoming the first driver with MS ever to race in any National Association for Stock Car Auto Racing (NASCAR) series, driving both cars and trucks.

To achieve this, a solution had to be found to still another challenge that was before Kelly. The challenge was the extreme heat that she and all NASCAR drivers are exposed to in their vehicles, where temperatures can soar to 120 degrees Fahrenheit. Heat can be very dangerous to a person who has MS. It can trigger many symptoms, including extreme fatigue and weakness in the legs, causing the person to lose their ability to walk.

But Kelly's dad, her strongest supporter, was not about to let this heat rob his little girl of her dreams. He focused on finding a solution and he found one. He had a cooling unit installed in her truck which pumped cool air into her driver's seat. It worked!

"Hey," the other drivers began saying, "I want one of those units!" The cooling unit that Kelly's dad had first introduced into her racing machine has now become popular with many NASCAR drivers.

"Racing has always been something I've been driven to do and I work hard to get to where I'm going," Kelly says. "I refuse to have things handed to me. I love getting behind the wheel and being in control of something on the verge of being out of control. I love the competition. I love the speed; I like the horsepower; I like everything about racing.

"My dad just has always taught me to be the best I can be, and that includes, you know, doing everything at your best. And, if you didn't do it good enough the first time, do it again. Try even harder. That's just the way I've been raised – to challenge myself most of all. And, I have always challenged myself.

"Racing is in my blood, it's who I am, and I refuse to let a diagnosis of MS take that from me," she says. "Interacting with other people who have MS reminds me that this disease is just something we have to deal with. It is not who we are. I am a mom; I am a racecar driver; I am an advocate. Those are the things that define me – not MS."

Kelly's bulldog determination earned her the 2003 Wilma Rudolph Courage Award from the Women's Sports Foundation. She has been honored with many awards, but Kelly says her most memorable award was not any one race she won but the honor of being named Metropolitan Auto Racing Fan Club of Maryland, Delaware and Virginia's Most Popular Driver. The reason this is such a special award for Kelly is that both her father and grandfather won the same award during their racing careers.

Awards are nice, but Kelly is more interested in using her notoriety to help others. For this reason, she launched her own Let It Shine Foundation to raise awareness and funds for people who have MS

www.ProveThemWrong.com

who lack the means to support themselves during relapses and crisis situations.

"I am so proud of Kelly for taking her diagnosis and turning it into something positive," says her mother. "Kelly cares about others who have MS, and she encourages them to pursue their dreams and to not let the disease rule their lives."

"The diagnosis does not mean you have to give up your dreams," Kelly says. "I believe that regardless of what challenge you're faced with in life, you need to focus on the positive. When you have a dream, focus on that. Put your energy on your dreams, not on your pain.

"First, never give up on yourself. And then, never give up on your dreams!"

To learn about or make donations to Kelly's Let It Shine Foundation, please visit www.LetItShineFoundation.com.

Kelly is also very passionate about raising funds for the Vietnam Veterans of America: www.VVA.org.

Kelly's father, who was always her hero and mentor, was a former U.S. Marine and a Vietnam veteran. He passed away on December 30, 2007. Kelly took some time off from racing to deal with this very sad loss. But now she is back! "I have set my eyes on the finish line, and I'm not stopping until I get there."

"No pessimist ever discovered the secret of the stars or sailed an uncharted land or opened a new doorway for the human spirit."

– Helen Keller

12
I Realized I Was Okay
Doug Grady

Doug was born in 1956 in Teaneck, New Jersey, a suburb of New York City. His four-year-old sister was thrilled to have a little brother. Though his sister could not hear, Doug was born with normal hearing.

However, when Doug was six months old, he, too, lost his hearing. This baffled his parents since, with the exception of his sister, there was no family history of hearing loss. There was no warning, no explanation. It just happened.

When Doug was one year old, his parents moved the family to Middletown, New Jersey, where he would live until he completed high school.

"I attended kindergarten at a local elementary school," Doug explains. "I was treated like a seemingly normal kid even though I didn't have any speech. Perhaps the teacher had already explained to the class that I was hearing impaired so the kids accepted me more readily. I began going to speech therapy when I was seven.

"I thought I spoke normally because I could never really quite hear myself talking. Before I was fitted with hearing aids at age six, I had never heard anything. My hearing loss was below 80 decibels [db], far beyond the conversation level at 30 db to 60 db."

However, Doug's hearing aids helped to capture only about one quarter of spoken words, and they had to be spoken slowly and clearly. It was nearly impossible for Doug to carry on a conversation since he could not hear the majority of what was being said.

"I never really liked to stay at the table during dinner; that was when my family talked about things. I found the conversations to be very boring so I would always be the first one to finish and then run to one other room to watch television. I never thought about being unable to understand the table conversations. My interests never included talking with people; I was someone that just wanted to do things to stay busy."

And stay busy he did. Doug loved sports. He joined a baseball team with the hope of making friends while also getting to play a sport at which he was pretty good. But the joy of playing baseball was mixed with the cruel teasing that is so common during childhood years.

"I started having problems when I was about ten," Doug remembers. "I can remember on my baseball team someone tricked me by offering me an unwrapped piece of Juicy Fruit gum. He was my teammate so I thanked him and put it in my mouth. He was laughing but I didn't know why. Then, later on, other kids were laughing at me. I found out from someone that the kid found the gum on the ground and I chewed it. I felt distraught as to why people were laughing at me.

"When I started junior high, I noticed that my old friends were ignoring me because they were making new friends at the school. Also, it was possible that they were embarrassed to have me around because I was different. I didn't make many new friends, and no one came to my locker to talk with me. I noticed, however, that I started to make friends through P.E. where I was good at sports."

These years were lonely years for Doug. With very little confidence in his ability to communicate with the hearing world, he spent a lot of time alone.

"As time went along, I became increasingly isolated at school. During my time in junior high, I somehow managed to find a way to make it through school. I was never invited over to someone's house once. I never talked on the phone, so I didn't really know what was going on in the social circle at school. This was a time where communication was a social necessity. Because I didn't have communication, I was feeling very insecure about myself.

"I was the only kid with a hearing problem at school. I was in a state of mind of trying to make up from the day before while all the other kids were moving on to the next day.

"I stopped going to the dances in junior high and I never went to one in high school. So, basically on Friday and Saturday nights, my friends were with their friends doing things and I was home alone watching TV. It was less painful being at home than being in the crowd and feeling left out.

"However, I was good in sports so I would go to the park to play golf every day or play tennis with people two or three or even four times my age on Saturday and Sunday mornings. Those were the things I could do without having to deal with communication. I knew I wasn't going to make any friends that way. I just let my athletic ability do the 'talking.'"

With so much emotional pain inside this young boy, who was growing into a young man, it would not be surprising if he just gave up. But would he give up?

"I had such low self-esteem that I never even thought about going to college. I didn't think I was good enough." But he was good enough, and he had begun to learn a valuable lesson. It's not what others think of you that's important – it's what you believe about yourself.

This young, intelligent man made up his mind that he was going to go to college. Upon graduating from high school, he enrolled at the Rochester Institute of Technology in 1974.

"It was going to college, meeting other deaf and hard of hearing people, when I realized I was okay. Some of the hard of hearing people knew sign language and some of the others did not. I did not know any sign language so I started to feel left out again! This time, it was with deaf people. However, I noticed some people not signing so I became friends with them. I connected with them quickly because they were someone like me! I seized the opportunity right away to make real friends, and I never felt more normal."

Doug went on to earn his Bachelor of Science degree in mechanical engineering in 1980. He began his career as a mechanical engineer and received his professional engineering license from the state of Texas in 1984.

Doug Grady, once a child who was grossly misunderstood and cast out of social circles because of his inability to communicate in the traditional sense, is today enjoying a successful engineering career with an aerospace firm in Tulsa, Oklahoma.

Giving up is not in his vocabulary. He looks ahead to what he wants to accomplish and he doesn't stop until he achieves it.

He also believes in playing an active role in community service. He served as President of the Board of Trustees for the Deaf Council of Greater Houston in 1986. He received an appointment from the governor of Texas to serve on the Texas Governor's Committee on People with Disabilities for eight years, and his primary focus was education for deaf children.

He is the proud father of two daughters, Shannon and Lauren, who are pursuing their own exciting careers. Mr. Grady has, without a doubt, achieved incredible success. His unshakeable determination to never give up, no matter how painful it may be to keep moving forward, has rewarded him with much deserved success. But the story doesn't end here.

On April 24, 2006, Mr. Grady received his first cochlear implant at Medical City Plaza in Dallas, Texas. A cochlear implant is a surgically implanted electronic device that allows a person with severe hearing loss to recognize some sounds.

He said, "It changed my life in a dramatic way. I didn't realize how important speech was. The cochlear implant enabled me to hear my own speech and I was able to hear all speech sounds. I guess it's part of human nature that my brain was able to adapt to the speech sounds and my speech improved dramatically."

In October of 2007, Mr. Grady received his second cochlear implant, also from Medical City Plaza.

For more information about Mr. Grady, his struggles with hearing loss, his attainment of a successful engineering career, and his new life with the cochlear implant, read *Hear Now* by Douglas Grady, and visit www.hearnow-with-cochlearimplant.com.

"By being open, you don't have to feel like you're hiding something. You don't have to feel inferior to your friends. You can be yourself and be open about it and move on and do what you're able to do."

– Alan Faneca, guard for the New York Jets, who happens to have epilepsy.

www.EpilepsyFoundation.org/aboutus/pressroom/pr20060202.cfm

13
Undaunted Determination
Sheri Denkensohn, J.D.

Life was peaceful growing up in the small rural town of Accord, New York – unlike the hustle and bustle of New York City, just two hours south. Reading a good book, going to the movies with friends, and sports filled Sheri's free time in this quiet and tranquil town.

"I was an energetic, physically active person, spending the summer of my sophomore year of high school employed as a lifeguard," Sheri describes. "I was eagerly awaiting the start of my junior year and was just about to begin summer practice for field hockey season. I felt like the world was at my fingertips."

It was a warm Monday evening, August 22, 1983. Sheri was sixteen years old. With still a few days left of summer vacation, Sheri was at a friend's house enjoying the backyard swimming pool.

There was a slide by the pool that provided an alternative choice for entering the cool, refreshing water. Being athletic and adventurous, Sheri decided to use the slide as a diving board. "I was sure the water was at least six feet deep," Sheri recalls. "It was not."

Sheri climbed up to the top of the slide and dived into the water, which was, in fact, only four feet deep. That is the last thing she remembers. Her head hit the bottom of the pool.

"I woke up a few days later," Sheri remembers, "on a Stryker frame bed in the intensive care unit with a ventilator in my mouth and prongs with weights attached to my head. I had no conception that I had sustained a cervical spinal cord injury and that I had officially become a quadriplegic. I remember slowly waking up in a hauntingly quiet room, with the exception of unfamiliar sounds emanating from the ventilator. As I opened my eyes, I saw my closest girlfriend looking at me through the window of the hospital room door. Neither one of us could utter a word, but the look in my friend's eyes spoke volumes. This was serious.

"I spent a month in the intensive care unit on the ventilator, and during that time my biggest fear was that I was never going to be able to talk again. I was an extremely verbal person and the inability to express myself felt even more disabling than the fact that I could not get out of bed. My mind would race with irrational thoughts because I could not verbally express my feelings. This experience was the first of many where I began to appreciate the ability to do things that I had always taken for granted. What sixteen-year-old imagines that someday she might not be able to talk?"

With half of Sheri's diaphragm also paralyzed, she would require extensive respiratory therapy to develop the strength to use the other half of her diaphragm to speak, as well as to breathe on her own without the use of a ventilator.

Ventilators? Therapists? Rehab centers? How quickly this young girl's world had changed.

"When I first heard that I was going to be transferred to a rehabilitation center, I actually believed that I was going to be spending the next few weeks at a specialized health club. In my mind I thought, 'Great. I will work out, get in shape and everything will be back to normal.' What I didn't realize is that going to the rehabilitation center was the first step in my adjustment to living life with a disability.

"I spent eight months at a rehabilitation center in Westchester County in New York. The center was two and a half hours away from my home town, so going there was somewhat like leaving for college at an early age. My family and friends came to visit on weekends, but during the week I would socialize with all of the other injured patients on my floor. I was the only spinal-cord-injured female on a floor with fifteen spinal-cord-injured men aged eighteen to forty-five. I was embraced by these men as one of 'the group,' but in reality I felt very alone. At that point I realized that it was up to me to learn how to adjust to what felt like a completely foreign existence. What I didn't yet know is that my strong sense of independence and undaunted determination would play a critical role in my adapting to life with a disability.

"I remember one really dark day in rehab when I was screaming at the nurses to help me end my life. I can't recall what the reason was, or whether it was just a buildup of frustration, but at that point I felt that I could not go on living with a disability. I wouldn't listen to anyone, especially one nurse who kept trying to talk to me and tell me that while things seemed dark, that I could live a good life. At that point, on that day, I didn't want to hear that I could experience a good quality of life living with a disability.

"But, as angry as I was, I made it through that day. I went on to achieve most of the goals set for me at rehab and fully developed every skill that I could based on my injury level. My determination continued to pull me through. It was now time to go home.

"Arriving back at my house after nine months away was an extremely painful experience. My wonderful and supportive family had installed a wheelchair lift so I could enter the house. In addition, they completely renovated a room on the first floor for me to use as a bedroom and bathroom because my former bedroom was up a long staircase. Being back home felt like a surreal experience – I was back in a familiar place but everything seemed totally unfamiliar. Nothing for me was the same and everything around me reminded me of my life prior to the injury. In that environment, I felt as if all of my limitations were accentuated."

Sheri's parents did all they could to make their home accessible for their youngest child. However, it was the 1980s, and the outside world was not so accessible.

"My parents ultimately purchased a wheelchair-accessible van, but shopping, restaurants and nightlife was located a distance away so I had to rely on my family or friends to drive me from place to place.

"With the help of very supportive teachers, I was tutored over the summer and was able to graduate from high school in 1985 with my class. I was chosen by my classmates to deliver the commencement address, and I spoke to my peers about being the 'captains of their own ship.' As the captain of my ship, I knew that I had to leave home. The environment was not conducive to my attaining independence. I knew in my heart that if I wanted to fully adapt to my disability, I had to live in a physical environment where I could begin to function more independently.

"The first step in achieving independence was attending college at the State University of New York at Albany. In August of 1985, only two years after sustaining my injury, I left home and moved into a dorm with four other women. Even though my roommates had no idea before we moved in together that I had a disability, all five of us got along famously. I began to realize that the qualities that contributed to my being well-liked by others before my injury remained unchanged. Also, the people that I met at college did not know me before my injury, so to them I was not 'different' from the way I used to be. I began to realize that people would continue to like me for who I was and that I was the one who had to work on becoming comfortable with my disability."

Sheri's college experience would be quite a bit different from that of her four roommates. While they could dash about campus on their own, Sheri needed a personal assistant with her much of the time.

"While my biggest life adjustment was that I could no longer independently perform activities of daily living, I faced the additional challenges of relearning basic skills that prior to my accident were second nature. One such skill was writing. Because I had no use of my hands, I utilized a splint on my arm to support my wrist, which meant that I had to adjust to writing with a pen placed into a device called a right angle pocket.

"Since I found that it was difficult to rely solely on the notes taken in class by my colleagues, I realized that to succeed in college I would have to learn to write fast enough to keep up with lectures. I started out writing very slowly and could barely read my own writing. After a few weeks, I found that I could keep up with the professor and that my penmanship had markedly improved. Conquering this obstacle was a major victory for me and made me confident that with determination I could overcome other significant barriers."

No obstacle too great, no barrier too large. This young woman was not going to allow anything to stand in her way of achieving her dreams, not even quadriplegia. Her determination paid off. Sheri earned her Bachelor of Science degree in business administration with a minor in political science. But now what?

Sheri's sister was fifteen years older than her and, though there were so many years separating these two, she served as a significant role model. Sheri's sister had graduated from law school and had already established a successful career as an attorney by the time Sheri had completed her undergraduate degree. Sheri was motivated to follow in her sister's footsteps and so enrolled in law school.

"My next challenge was succeeding in law school and adjusting to living in a new city. After graduating from college, I began the night student program at the Georgetown University Law Center in Washington D.C. My sister and her family lived in the D.C. area, and through my exposure to the area I felt that Washington would be a very desirable place for me to live because of the climate and accessibility. Again, this transition did not occur without difficulty.

"Hiring personal assistants, handling the heavy course load of law school and managing chronic health issues posed significant challenges. To my surprise, as each year passed, my outlook on life improved. I adapted to the rigors of law school. I found a cadre of qualified doctors and addressed some of my significant medical issues. I was able to hire extremely reliable personal care assistants. And, most importantly I found an accessible apartment in a neighborhood that offered a variety of services that I could utilize independently. For the first time since acquiring my disability, I felt empowered and in control of my own life."

In 1991, while in law school, Sheri applied and was hired for a part-time job at a Federal Office of Inspector General. She has continued to work for several Offices of Inspector General since her graduation from law school in 1993. Sheri presently serves as Special Assistant to the Inspector General at the U.S. Department of Health and Human Services.

"I have become increasingly independent since graduating from law school in 1993. As an attorney for the federal government, I have found success and fulfillment in my career. I have achieved career goals that I believe I would have set for myself even if I did not have a disability.

"I have also found meaning in working with organizations that support the interests of individuals with disabilities. Being active in these organizations has afforded me the opportunity to work on issues that impact the lives of individuals with disabilities who lack the family support and resources necessary to live meaningful and independent lives. My participation in these organizations has also helped me to more fully develop my own identity as a woman with a disability."

In 2003, during Sheri's sixth year serving as a member of the board for the local Independent Living Center, she met Tony, a new employee at the center. Tony had just bought season tickets for the

Georgetown University Hoyas. "Not only was I also a basketball fan," Sheri said, "but Georgetown was my favorite team!"

Tony invited Sheri to one of the games and that would be their first date of many. On New Year's Eve, 2004, Tony proposed to Sheri and on September 3, 2005, Sheri and Tony were married.

Is this the same person who, in 1983, did not want to go on living? It is definitely the same person who said, "My determination continued to pull me through."

When asked what the key to her success has been, Sheri is quick to answer, "Education, education, education. Value education and, despite obstacles that may stand in your way, that needs to be a priority. Education is the key."

Sheri continues, "In addition, become an advocate for yourself. Get involved in organizations and learn to advocate for yourself. Take charge of yourself. With education, advocacy, and personal empowerment you can make a difference for yourself and others."

"Take what you've got and find a way to make it work for you."

– Ray Charles

www.youtube.com/watch?v=ghz4_kikLkE

14
I Couldn't, But I Could
Tony Melendez

"We are filled with doubt. Today is like no other day before. You and I will never be the same."

But why? It should have been a time for new hope. It should have been a time to celebrate. A baby boy had just been born to Mr. and Mrs. Melendez. Their only other child, two-year-old José, now had a little brother.

When Mrs. Melendez began experiencing the early signs of pregnancy, they were confused with symptoms of the flu. Her family doctor prescribed a new drug called Thalidomide which had recently been imported to Nicaragua where the Melendez family lived.

As babies began being born with severe deformities, researchers began questioning the safety of Thalidomide being taken by pregnant women. Just a few months after Mrs. Melendez had taken just one Thalidomide pill, a massive recall of the drug was sounded around the world. But it was too late to protect the newest member of the Melendez family.

A son, Tony, was born on January 9, 1962. No one had ever heard of or seen such a baby.

Baby Tony had been born with no hands and no arms. He had one tiny finger growing out of his left shoulder. He did not have the normal ten toes but instead had eleven, with the extra toe growing out of the side of his left foot. His lower left leg

was deformed, and his left foot was a club foot which was twisted back up against his left leg.

After several moments of tears and painful thoughts, Tony's mother began drawing her strength from her faith in God. She cradled baby Tony in her arms and, ignoring the damaged and missing parts of his body, she began telling him about all that God had given him.

"Other people saw me as I was," Tony says, "a tiny, crippled, armless child. But my mother saw me as I one day would be, a grown man with God's dream in my heart. She believed with all her heart that God had a wonderful purpose for my life."

After a doctor advised that Tony could get better medical care in the United States, the Melendez family traveled 5,000 miles north to stay with family members in Los Angeles, California, arriving seven days after Tony's first birthday. With the March of Dimes stepping up to pay for Tony's medical bills, surgeries to straighten Tony's club foot began in late 1963.

It would be the summer of 1964 before the last cast would be removed from Tony's foot and leg, which meant it was finally time for Tony, now two and a half years old, to begin to learn to walk. But what happens when a toddler, as he's learning to walk, doesn't have arms to catch himself when he falls? Needless to say, Tony's chin was busted open countless times from falling face first into furniture.

"But I did learn to walk," Tony explains, "and, after working with an orthopedic specialist, I learned a better way to fall, by tucking my shoulder and somersaulting over."

From the beginning, Tony was doing things with his toes and feet that other children do with their fingers and hands. Tony describes, "I could wedge a crayon between my toes and draw some very decorated pictures. I could build things with my

building blocks and figured out ways to play with every kind of toy that I saw my older brother being entertained with."

By the time Tony was four years old he had two younger sisters and his family was getting ready to move to Chino, a suburb of Los Angeles, where Tony's dad's job would now be.

Tony was enrolled in the Cypress Orthopedic School. He longed to attend public school like his older brother but everyone else believed he needed to be in a school for students who had a disability.

"I was fitted with an artificial arm," Tony remembers. "They decided to start with just one arm and I absolutely hated it. This mechanical arm was heavy, clumsy, and difficult to move. Sometimes this arm would get stuck in different positions and I had to wait until someone would come to my rescue and put my arm down. I didn't like to raise my hand in class to answer a question because it might get stuck in the air."

"Sometimes on the playground," Tony continued, "kids would tease me by pulling my arm out like it was a wing and it would get stuck like that. I'd have to walk around on the playground with my arm out until someone would come to my rescue. So," Tony laughs as he recalls, "every chance I got, I managed to hide or lose this arm. I knew my feet would be my hands and my toes would be my fingers."

If only he could convince others of that. Stubborn, lazy, stupid, and short-sighted were just a few of the words Tony was called by people trying to insist that he wear a mechanical arm. But why?

"I could play jacks with my sisters, tossing the ball with one foot and picking up the jacks with the other foot," Tony recalls. "I dressed myself by tossing a shirt onto my bed with one foot, buttoning the buttons with my toes, and then tossing it into the air and ducking under it as it parachuted down."

With practice, he learned to squirm into pants and he wore sandals, so no need to tie or lace shoes. With practice, his toes got stronger and more accurate. "I could pick up the key to my house with my toes and unlock the door," Tony continues. "I could dial the phone with my big toe, turn on the television, start the water in the shower or tub, turn pages in my school books, and pack my backpack for school. I figured out ways to brush my teeth, brush my hair, and apply soap in the shower."

Eventually his therapists began to believe him, that maybe the mechanical arm really was not needed after all. Tony was thirteen years old when he was finally allowed to put the mechanical arm away for good.

"I couldn't use a bicycle but I could flip a skateboard onto my shoulder, walk to the nearest sidewalk, and skateboard to anywhere I wanted to go," Tony explains. "I couldn't play the violin or trumpet but I discovered I could play an electronic organ. I couldn't play football or baseball but I can swim and play soccer."

As Tony grew, it became more obvious that this young boy could do a lot more than anyone ever expected of him. His dream of going to public school finally became reality as he entered his freshman year of high school. But this young teenager would once again be disappointed.

He was enrolled in the "handicapped program," as it was called in those days, and basically cut off from the other kids. Frustrated that he was not being challenged intellectually, Tony demanded that he be moved into "normal" classes.

"I was going nuts in that class," Tony remembers. "I had to get out. I had to prove that I could make it in the 'normal' classes, proving that I could then make it in the 'normal' world."

Finally, he was taken out of the program for students with disabilities and was soon placed in the honors classes. His intelligence was finally being recognized. He tried out for and made his high school's soccer team and was just as successful as his teammates. "You don't need arms to play soccer," Tony explains, "and I knew how to use my head, legs, and feet."

Next, Tony joined his high school's choir and soon his choir director was spotlighting his singing talent. "Music was a big part of my life," Tony says. "It always had been since I was very young and I would listen to my dad singing and playing his guitar."

When Tony was fifteen years old, he grasped his dad's guitar between his neck and shoulder and carried it into his bedroom and placed the guitar at his feet. Attempting to form chords with his left foot, he strummed the strings with the toes of his right foot. It sounded terrible!

Tony shared his unsuccessful tries with a guitarist from his church. He advised Tony to tune his guitar to an open chord. Now tuned to a G major chord, it sounded good when Tony strummed his big toe across the strings. As he put his other foot up or down the fret a new chord would form. Next he learned to hold a pick between the two largest toes on his right foot.

During his last three years of high school, Tony practiced on his dad's guitar four or five hours a day. He was soon invited to accompany the church choir, to perform at weddings, funerals, and church services.

If he wasn't busy enough with music, sports and honors classes, add to that a part-time job after school, and I guess you could say that Tony was just your typical, everyday, American teenaged boy.

We all know, of course, that teenagers consider one of their most important achievements during this age to be getting their driver's license. And Tony was no exception. With the steering wheel mounted on the floor, he uses a foot control system that allows him to steer the wheel with his left foot while his right foot works the brake and accelerator. Impossible? Don't use that word with Tony. It's not in his vocabulary.

His dream, for as long as he could remember, was always to become a priest in the Catholic Church. And now, as he grew into a young man, it was time to take action on this dream. "Your application to enter the priesthood has been rejected by the church." Tony listened in disbelief as the church leader spoke these crushing words to him. "They are saying that you must have a thumb and index finger in order to administer the Eucharist."

This wasn't the first time Tony had been told that he didn't belong, that he wasn't good enough, and that he was too different to be included. But this time was different, for this time was going to affect the rest of his life.

After graduating from high school, Tony was having trouble getting a job. No one would hire him because he had no arms. "I began playing my guitar on the streets of Laguna Beach, California. With my guitar case open for people to drop their money in, I would play songs I had composed about my faith in God."

Though he loved sharing his songs about his faith, he admitted to his friend that he felt like a beggar sharing his music this way.

When Tony was twenty-one years old, his father, the man Tony had loved and had learned so much from, passed away. Tony needed a way to help his mother pay the bills and playing for donations seemed to be the only way. Frustration and doubt crept into Tony's mind. "What will I do with my life?" Tony wondered.

At a time when everything was looking so hopeless, Tony received a letter in the mail from a man who was inviting him to audition to perform for Pope John Paul II during his 1987 tour of the United States. After his audition, the committee unanimously agreed that Tony's performance was the musical gift they wanted to present to the Pope.

The day arrived – September 15, 1987. Tony arrived at the Universal Ampa Theatre in Hollywood, California. 6,000 people, mostly youth, were sitting in the theatre anxiously awaiting the arrival of the Pope. This event was being televised to a worldwide audience of over one billion people.

The moment arrived. Tony was introduced and the spotlight was put on him. The Pope and the audience saw for the first time this young man sitting on a chair with his guitar lying at his feet. Tony began to strum the strings with his toes. The audience quieted as Tony began to sing a song he had composed entitled *Never Be the Same*:

We are filled with doubt
Today is like no other day before
You and I will never be the same

I give you all my love
This day and every day, forever and forever
In our joys and in our pain

We become the kind of love our God has given us
We become the witness to his grace

We fill the day with love
Today is like no other day before, and even more
You and I will never be the same

To see this breathtaking performance for yourself, visit www.youtube.com/watch?v=fC60dBXTfvQ&feature=related.

For more information about Tony, his music, and his performances, visit www.TonyMelendez.com.

Excerpts taken, with permission, from the best-seller *A Gift of Hope,* by Tony Melendez.

"Never let what you can't do get in the way of what you can."

– Heidi VanArnem, founder of ICAN

www.techdivas.com/heidivanarnum.htm

15
I Don't Waste the Energy
Kathryn Woodcock, Ph.D.

"Each September, I presented myself to each teacher with the little note from my mother with the dirty secret: 'Kathryn has a hearing problem. Please let her sit in the front row,'" Kathryn explains. By the time Kathryn was ten years old, the hearing loss was enough to affect her ability to grasp everything being said.

Kathryn said, "I generally comprehended by lip-reading even before my first hearing test at age thirteen. I wouldn't hear some words and not others – I would hear some sounds such as vowels but not the consonants that make those noises into sensible words. I wouldn't miss one or two words – I would be following along fine with rhythm, hearing mainly vowels, and lip-reading, and then totally lose the thread of the conversation. Worst case scenario, I would not realize that I had lost the thread and I would THINK I was understanding, when in fact I was not."

"Neither surgery or hearing aids will improve your daughter's hearing," doctors explained to Kathryn's parents. It was the 1960s. No matter how many appointments this young girl had with specialists, the prognosis never changed. "There's nothing we can do to help Kathryn."

Kathryn remembers, "I went through high school and university sitting in the front row and surviving with lip-reading as my hearing loss crept into the lower frequencies. By the time I was in the last year of university, I had no hearing at all above 1100 hertz."

Kathryn continues, "I was NEVER 'not expected to amount to much.' EVERYONE around me expected me to do anything and everything, including hearing, if I tried harder."

Trying harder was not going to restore Kathryn's hearing. But this young girl was growing into a young woman who understood the value of hard work and persistence. She had also developed her own system for breaking down the barriers that stood between her and her career goals.

Kathryn Woodcock earned her bachelor's and master's degrees in systems design engineering from the University of Waterloo in Waterloo, Ontario, Canada. At the young age of twenty-four, she was hired to serve as vice president of a large hospital in Toronto where she was responsible for a $20 million budget and 600 employees in six departments.

It was near the end of her tenure at this hospital that Kathryn met, for the first time, another person who was deaf. She said, "I started to learn sign language when I was about thirty, and I don't waste the energy on lip-reading as much as I used to when I didn't have the choice."

Kathryn then went on to become the first woman who is deaf to earn a Ph.D. in engineering, earning this doctorate from the University of Toronto. Recalling the high expectations others had of her, Dr. Woodcock said, "Being a hospital VP at the age of twenty-four and getting a Ph.D. was absolutely within the realm of expectation."

Today, Dr. Woodcock is an associate professor in the School of Occupational and Public Health at Ryerson University, teaching courses in occupational safety and ergonomics, and is the principal investigator at the THRILL lab, where she does research and develops applications of human factors engineering to amusement ride safety.

Dr. Woodcock is the author of the book, *Deafened People: Adjustment and Support*, which was published by the University of Toronto Press.

She is highly respected for her engineering expertise as well as for her first-hand knowledge of living with a disability, and has served on numerous industry, professional and community boards and committees. She has presented papers and lectured internationally on ergonomics, safety, and reasonable accommodations.

She created The Deafened People Page in 1996: www.deafened.org. This is a site for people who are deafened, also referred to as late deafened or having acquired deafness. It is a non-profit resource and research entity.

She has received many prestigious honors and awards for her work, both as an engineer and for her community service and advocacy.

The young girl who was once misunderstood because of her inability to hear is, today, a well-respected university professor, engineer, lecturer, consultant, trainer, educator, author, and advocate.

For more information about Dr. Kathryn Woodcock, please visit www.ryerson.ca/woodcock/about/personal/book/.

A reporter asked Tom Dolan how many more Olympic medals he could have won if he had not had asthma. Tom answered:

"Maybe I wouldn't have won any. Maybe I wouldn't have known how to overcome adversity. I wouldn't have known what I had in me."

– Tom Dolan, Olympic Gold Medalist, inducted into the International Swimming Hall of Fame in 2006

16
Keep Focusing on the Top of Your Mountain
Richard Turner

Every Sunday evening at 6:30 PM, Richard would pull his chair up to the family's black and white television set to watch his favorite show, *Maverick*, a western action series about an adventurous gambler roaming from town to town looking for poker games. The year was 1961. Richard was seven years old.

Richard loved to act out what he saw Maverick doing with his cards each week. With playing cards in hand, he would challenge his imaginary friends to a poker game. Richard would shuffle the cards, then deal them to each player while always making sure the aces were stacked in his favor. These imaginary card games could continue for hours, often interrupted only when this clever gambling cowboy's mother told him it was time to go to bed.

Richard loved cards. He could spend hours sitting by himself shuffling, cutting, dealing, all the time figuring out ways to do each to his advantage. Life was good growing up with his three younger siblings, Debra, Lori, and Mike, in El Cajon, California, a suburb of San Diego. However, when Richard was nine years old and his sister Lori was six, they both came down with scarlet fever, essentially a special term for a strep throat which has a scarlet-colored rash associated with it.

Soon after recovering from this illness, Richard noticed a change in his vision. He could no longer see what his fourth grade teacher was writing on the chalkboard. "Why can't I see the print in my school books?" Richard wondered. "Everything is so blurry. This is so strange."

Richard's parents wasted no time in taking their oldest child to the eye doctor. "The macula," the doctor explained, "which is what gives us our central or most detailed vision, has been destroyed in the retina nerve in both of Richard's eyes. He does have some peripheral or side vision, although a lot of damage has also been done to that as well."

Richard's sister, Lori, also lost her sight soon after recovering from scarlet fever. Because of this, the family believed the blindness must have been caused by the illness. However doctors, to this day, are still not certain of the cause.

At school, instruction for Richard came to a screeching halt. Because he could no longer see the print in his books, he was not expected to do the same work as his classmates. "Most of my time at school was filled with art projects," Richard remembers, "and that was fine with me because I loved art and was good at it."

He received a great deal of praise from his teachers for his artwork. However, his classmates were not so generous with the praise. "Look," one would tease, "he's sitting so close to the canvas that he's got paint on his nose." Laughter would erupt. The teacher would step in, but not before the words cut Richard like a newly-sharpened blade.

Yet, there was still another challenge waiting around the corner. At age ten, he was diagnosed as having asthma.

This young, talented, sweet boy began to see himself as the schoolyard bullies saw him – scrawny, blind, and asthmatic. It was not uncommon for the bullies to torment Richard to the point of his ending up in tears, adding even more embarrassment to the situation. His self-image was quickly diminishing.

Believing that their son was not being challenged academically because of his loss of sight, his parents made the difficult decision to send their son to Carlton Hills, a school that specialized in educating students who are blind and visually impaired, in Santee, California.

"What is to become of me and my life?" Richard worried as he realized the major change he was about to undergo. "Am I so different that I can't even attend the same middle school as my friends?"

He entered the sixth grade at his new school. His new classmates were, like him, visually impaired. However, Richard still had a difficult time fitting in. There was, though, one classmate named Ruben who enjoyed the entertainment Richard could provide with his playing cards. Ruben would select a card, hold it close to his eyes to see the card, and then return it to the deck. To his amazement, Richard could find the card every time. Unfortunately, the success Richard had with his playing cards was not being carried over into the other areas of his life.

As he progressed through his middle school years, something was changing inside this once sensitive and caring young boy. By the time he reached the eighth grade, he no longer cared about school. He didn't even care about himself. As though a firecracker had just been lit, Richard's rebellious years were ignited, and there would be no turning back for nearly four years.

He adopted many unhealthy choices for his life – choices that nearly took his young life, and did take the lives of many of his teenaged peers who adopted the same lifestyle. Upon completion of the eighth grade, Richard moved to El Cajon High School, not his neighborhood school, but rather the only high school in the district with a program for students with a visual impairment.

His desire to blend in and not stand out from the crowd was short-lived. On the first day of school he had a bad asthma attack that got him a great deal of unwanted attention. He was able to return to class after lunch, but this first day of school would not end before getting in trouble for playing cards in history class, attempting to swindle a classmate out of his lunch money.

The weeks and months that followed proved that his defiant behavior was at full throttle. He was expelled from high school. He was reinstated two months later on the condition that he see a psychiatrist once a week.

In time, he was drawn to the high school's drama and theater programs, where he acted in several of the school's productions. Unfortunately, those successes were often accompanied by more defiant behavior, mixing accolades for his acting talent with punishment for his unacceptable behavior.

Richard was growing weary of living like this. He began to recognize that he had given up on all his childhood dreams. He began to recognize how he had turned away from everything he had been taught as a small child in his Sunday school lessons.

"On February thirteenth of my junior year in high school," Richard said, "I happened upon three young people who were reading the Bible. We talked for several hours. Before I got up to leave, I was a changed person. I vowed I would piece my life back together again."

But his power to press forward in the face of devastating tragedy would soon be put to the test. He had always been close to his sister, Debra, who was two years younger than him. One afternoon as she was walking home from school, she was struck and killed by a drunk driver. She was just fourteen years old. Richard, sixteen years old at the time, could not understand why such a tragedy had to happen. He grieved for months.

Despite his very sad and painful loss, he held steadfast to his decision to turn his life around and aggressively pursue his boyhood dreams. But there were still many questions on his mind. "How can I ever make a living for myself? I can't see and I have no real talent," Richard thought to himself.

Even though he had more questions than answers, Richard began making plans for his future. The first step, he believed, was to improve his health. The asthma medications he had tried did more harm than good, and he knew he would need to control his asthma with better nutrition and exercise.

His little brother, David, had been taking karate lessons for several months, and Richard was impressed when he saw David break a board with his bare hands. "I wish I could do that," Richard fantasized out loud.

"You can," David assured him, "You just have to train to learn how to do it."

An instructor at the karate school, John Douglas, told John Murphy, the karate master and owner of the school, "I've got a visually impaired kid who can barely see two feet in front of his face, but he still wants to train. Do you think we can work with him?"

Murphy replied, "If he's got the heart and can see shadows, we'll take him."

Richard began karate lessons in 1971 under the guidance of Master John Murphy. The first job at hand was to establish a fitness regimen to increase Richard's strength and body mass. Weight training, push-ups, sit-ups, punching bag workouts, running, and kicking exercises, coupled with relentless karate training, slowly began to transform this thin and frail teenaged boy, who was once terrified of getting hit, into a strong and confident young man. And more wonderful opportunities were waiting for Richard.

In 1972, now a freshman in college, Richard was invited to audition for an acting role with a small Christian theater company called Lamb's Players, which would go on to become an award-winning company. It was operated by television actor Steve Terrell. Richard not only got the part but he remained an actor with this company for six years.

This experience helped to develop Richard's communication skills. Despite not being able to see the person he was speaking to, Richard was trained to follow voices in order to look people in the eye. More importantly, Mr. Terrell said something to Richard that, to this day, Richard lives by. He said, "If you want to be respected, you have to be the best at what you do. Only then will people be willing to listen to whatever you have to say."

Richard took this advice to heart, not only in his acting with the Lamb's Players, but also in his karate training and, more importantly, in mastering skills with his playing cards. He would practice with his cards up to sixteen hours a day, every single day. It was rare to find Richard without a deck of cards in his hands. He was constantly picking up new card ideas from books and from other card mechanics.

A card mechanic is someone who gains advantage in a card game by arranging the cards through sleight of hand, and this was exactly what Richard was becoming. He was becoming quite smooth at dealing off the bottom of the deck and even the most difficult of all, dealing the aces from the middle of the pack.

Once a very troubled young teenaged boy, he had now discovered his passion. He loved to entertain and he loved doing things with a deck of cards that no one else could do. As he persisted in mastering what was considered to be difficult and even impossible by the expert card mechanics, Richard was gaining respect both locally and nationally, and later, internationally.

He was invited to be a guest at the Magic Castle, a magic club in Hollywood, California, where only professional magicians are accepted as members. While there, he met Professor Dai Vernon, a legendary card mechanic, who was impressed with Richard's hunger to be the very best. He began to mentor and teach Richard.

"I felt privileged and blessed beyond belief to have had that great and rare honor to have been the professor's private pupil," Richard said.

There was a riverboat in San Diego called the Reuben E. Lee, and Richard's goal was to get a job on that boat entertaining the passengers with his card mechanics. He ultimately got that job and he performed aboard the riverboat for seven years. That long-term engagement landed him high-profile appearances on many major TV shows, features in newspapers and magazines, and invitations to entertain at celebrity and corporate parties.

More importantly, however, while working on this riverboat Richard met Kim, the love of his life, who was the assistant general manager of the boat. They married on November 21, 1992. Their son, Asa Spades, was born in 1995.

Today Mr. Turner is president of his own company called Showdown Creations, Inc. He has produced the DVD series titled *Richard Turner, The Cheat*, which is one of the most comprehensive video series on card table techniques. He has designed and created a series of board games, puzzles, and electronic gambling games, including Texas Showdown and Batty. And, of course, he has designed his own deck of cards called Gambler's Playing Cards.

He holds the record for coin rolling, in which he can roll eight coins around one hand, something no one else to this date has been able to do. He has been inducted into the Magic Castle Hall of Fame and has been a performing member since 1975. His unique card handling ability and incredibly sensitive fingertips so impressed the United States Playing Card Company that they employ his services as a "touch analyst" to evaluate the texture, flexibility and cut of dozens of decks of cards each year.

This man, who as a child saw himself as a scrawny, blind, asthmatic kid, is today a fifth degree black belt in karate. Once a child who wondered how he would ever be able to work with no eyesight and no real talent, he grew up to be called the most skillful card mechanic in the world. Mr. Turner said, "My best wasn't good enough. I had to be better than anybody else."

He said his key to success has been his focused passion. He doesn't allow anything to distract him from his goal. His advice to others is "Keep focused. Don't look to the left or right, just keep focusing on the top of your mountain. Take one thing and focus on it and don't stop until you are over the top. Hear what people are saying but don't let that distract you from your goal.

If it doesn't directly give you a step toward your goal then let it roll off your back and keep going."

To see Richard Turner in action with his cards, visit the following link and click on the link that says "Download 12 minute video." www.RichardTurner52.com/performances/

To learn more about Richard Turner, please visit www.RichardTurner52.com

"My wheelchair does not confine me. It takes me places I otherwise could never go."

– Unknown

17
It Fueled My Fire to Become the Best
I felt I Could Become
Chris Glavin

"You'll never amount to anything in life," were words Chris heard often, especially from his third grade teacher.

"I think my major problem while I was in school was gaining a focus on all of my subjects," Chris said. "Many times I found more interest in a subject not related to the current school work. I was in the public school system from kindergarten to third grade. While I was there the teachers had a lot of trouble keeping me focused on the subjects at hand."

It was 1986; Chris was four years old when he was diagnosed as having attention deficit disorder, also known as ADD. A person with ADD may have extreme difficulty paying attention, focusing, following directions, organizing, and completing certain mundane tasks. However, they are often able to focus intently on activities in which they are keenly interested.

"While I consider it to be a blessing in disguise," Chris explains, "part of having ADD is having the ability to hyper-focus on a subject of interest. When you are hyper-focused, you tend to push aside and block out other areas of interest that are important. Lucky for me I was always into computers, and once I entered high school I found it to be a passion in life. I was lucky enough to go to one of the best prep schools in Pennsylvania, which also had one of the best computer programs in the country."

Though high school presented many exciting new opportunities for Chris, his early elementary school years had not been so rewarding.

"I can always remember teachers telling me how much trouble I was," Chris remembers. "My third grade teacher wanted to place me in a classroom with children who had mental disabilities. The only reason they did not do this was because I always had good grades."

Unable to stay focused on the specific lesson being taught, Chris's behavior was often misunderstood as an inability to learn. But he could learn. He just had a different style of learning.

"There were a handful of teachers who saw that I had potential in life, and really went above and beyond the call of duty to help me. However, there were those in my earlier, formative years in life who told me I would not succeed – it fueled my fire to become the best I felt I could become. I also felt a responsibility as somebody who has ADD to show that you can succeed in life.

"I ran the official fan club and website while in high school for comedian and former host of *E! Entertainment Television Talk Soup*, John Henson. I ran a website which covered the entire national pro wrestling scene on the independent level. I feel my one true success is proving all my critics wrong. Statistics show that only a small percentage of individuals complete high school with ADD. I completed high school at one of the best Catholic schools in Pennsylvania, LaSalle College High School."

Today, Chris has taken what he loves, designing and managing websites, and coupled it with education, something he has always valued, yet something that has been more difficult for him to obtain than most. In 2005, at age twenty-three, Chris Glavin opened his own business called K12 Academics, which he describes as "Your definitive education resource website for the United States." Within eight months of opening this business, he made it his full-time job. Since 2008, the website for K12 Academics has been considered a resource by the U.S. Department of Education and the U.S. Library of Congress.

Mr. Glavin, once a child who was not expected to succeed, today is the CEO of a successful national business which has a client base of well over 2,000 schools, businesses, organizations, programs, camps, and colleges. His business website is in the top 100,000 websites in the United States, receiving more than one million hits per month.

Mr. Glavin says, "I feel those who have ADD truly have a blessing in life. It is also a crutch, but if the right people are put into place and these individuals received the right attention, then they can become more successful than any other student in their class. We have the ability to hyper-focus on things that we enjoy, and because of this we do it better than anybody else can.

"So many kids with ADD tend to lead to drugs and crime. So few graduate. I attended a school for children with learning disabilities which helped me become the success I am today. The school is The Woodlynde School in Stafford, Pennsylvania. I went there during middle school. They paid special attention to my needs.

"I also had a great child psychologist, Dr. Tom Powers of the Children's Seashore House in Philadelphia, Pennsylvania, who helped me focus on all my tasks at hand, and helped me to see the positives in my disability. I cannot speak highly enough for this school and Dr. Powers.

"ADD/ADHD can be very difficult and straining on a family. It was the loving patience, determination and continued support of my parents that is the reason why I am the success that I am today."

To see the outstanding educational resource this young businessman has created, visit www.k12academics.com.

"Find something you love and go after it with all of your heart."

– Jim Abbott, a former major league baseball pitcher who is best known for playing despite being born without a right hand.

www.jimabbott.info

To see Jim Abbott in action, visit
www.youtube.com/watch?v=xOU5dogqhGc

18
I Just Went Ahead with My Plan
Betty Davidson, Ph.D.

She held the beetle in her small hand, studying this six-legged insect. It seemed so small, so fragile. Yet, it had everything it needed, from flight wings to legs that, when not used for walking, could be modified and adapted for other uses, such as swimming, digging, and jumping.

"That's so amazing," Betty thought. And beetles came in such beautiful colors and patterns! Brilliant reds and yellows, metallic blues and greens! Stripes! Squiggles! Spots! She could admire beetles all day long!

"When I was a child," Betty said, "I loved to read and just sit in one place, usually the empty lot on the corner, and observe. I grew up in Coney Island, a Brooklyn neighborhood very near the water – actually right at the entrance to New York Harbor. The empty lot was a sandy piece of shore land. There were all kinds of beach plants and many different insects living there. I spent a lot of time just lying there and observing the comings and goings of the ants, beetles and caterpillars, and admiring the butterflies."

Fascinated with these tiny creatures, Betty made her way to this empty corner lot every chance she got. "I got myself down to the empty lot on our corner," Betty describes, "by walking bent over, holding my left knee straight, so it would support my weight."

Betty was born with club feet and contracted knees. Club feet is a condition in which the child is born with the feet turned inwards and pointing down, making it very difficult to walk. "Contracted knees," Betty describes, "are knees that are permanently bent, as in a sitting position, and unable to straighten out."

But the beetle in Betty's hand didn't notice her misshaped feet and legs. It walked to the end of her finger and then jumped, landing back on the sandy ground, ready to return to its natural habitat.

Betty's young mind was full of questions. "Where do these insects live? What do they eat? What happens if I plug up the opening to the anthill?" The ants seemed to cooperate and work together. At other times, swarms of ants seemed to be fighting with each other. All that fascinated her. How did they know to do those things? Were they communicating with each other?

Back at her house, Betty was being home-schooled. She longed to attend public school like all the neighbor kids, but instead she had a teacher coming to her house three times a week for two-hour lessons.

"The reason given for my home schooling," Betty remembers, "was that there was too much interruption for surgeries, of which I had many throughout my childhood." These surgeries would correct Betty's club feet and allow her contracted knees to be more functional.

"I was ten years old before the number of surgeries I needed slowed down, and it was at that time that I got my first pair of crutches," Betty said. "Before someone thought to get me crutches, I used no mobility aids and had extremely limited mobility. Now, with a pair of crutches and fewer interruptions from surgeries, I was finally allowed to go to public school. I was very excited. Although I learned a lot working at home, it was lonely with no one my age to talk to."

Entering school for the first time as a fifth grader, Betty quickly discovered that public school was not what she had imagined it to be. It was 1943. Betty was ten years old, and the treatment which students with disabilities endured during that generation was dreadful.

Betty recalls, "School was a segregated classroom. It was called the 'handicapped' class. It was in the corner of the basement in an elementary school. We weren't allowed to mingle with the other children, the ones who did not have a disability, except for during the weekly assembly.

"My classroom had students from the fifth to the eighth grades, with only one teacher and no aides. The teacher only taught the basic subjects – reading, writing, and arithmetic. That's all she had time for. Because everyone was in a different grade level, we had to just sit and wait for the teacher to teach those subjects for our grade. While we waited for our turn, we played a lot of board games. We also helped our classmates with their writing if they had poor motor control, and we tutored those who needed help with spelling or arithmetic."

While students in the so-called "normal" classrooms were learning and being challenged, the students who had a disability were moving at a snail's pace with a minimal education.

"Nobody seemed to have any expectations for my life," Betty remembers. "As a child, I couldn't imagine what I was going to be when I grew up. I don't remember even thinking about it until high school. I was told all the time and in many ways that I would never be able to succeed. It seemed that all my aspirations always elicited the same response: 'Not For You.'

"I was born in 1933. Back then everyone assumed that children born with a disability could not lead the same lives as other people. It seemed that everyone believed this, from teachers to doctors to social workers. That is what they told parents of kids who had a disability. I think that most parents, and many of the children, believed it too. That's just the way it was in the thirties and forties.

Until I was twelve years old, I also believed it. I certainly had no dream or any picture of what I could become.

"Then I got into high school. I went to the same classes as everyone else, and I found out that there was such a thing as biology and chemistry and I loved learning about it." The fascination and sense of wonder that had lured the eight-year-old Betty to the empty lot to look at the bugs, butterflies and plants, now evolved into a true passion.

"In high school I found out that I could excel, even in the laboratory, and I decided that in college I would major in a science. Luckily, my parents, even though they had no expectations that I would ever have a job, felt strongly that I would at least have an education. It was always assumed that I would go to college, as my parents, aunts, and uncles all had done. When I entered college, my parents were horrified that I was planning to major in chemistry. They felt that I would not be able to do the labs. But by then, I knew that they were mistaken, so I just went ahead with my plan."

Betty's parents, though still unsure about their young daughter's future, could not have been more proud of their only child. The determination and persistence that Betty had used to get her to the empty lot without the use of mobility aids when she was a child was now moving her across the very large Brooklyn College campus.

"I think college was my turning point. The whole world really opened to me, not only in science, but also with arts and

humanities, as well as socially. It was the first time I felt really happy in my skin."

Betty earned a Bachelor of Science degree in chemistry from Brooklyn College. But she didn't stop there. She went on to earn a Ph.D. in biochemistry from the University of Chicago! It was at the University of Chicago that Betty met and married Jim, who, like Betty, was also a biochemist. They were married for twenty-eight years before he passed away in 1988. They raised two wonderful sons who have each gone on to live their dreams in their chosen careers, the older as a lawyer and the younger as a physical therapist.

Today Dr. Davidson is a well-respected scientist with fifteen years of biochemical research experience. Following her work as a researcher, Dr. Davidson accepted a position with the Museum of Science in Boston, Massachusetts, where she worked as exhibit planner for fifteen years.

A leading expert in the field of museum exhibit accessibility, Dr. Davidson has made a lasting contribution to informal science education by developing inclusive, hands-on exhibits that excite and intrigue all museum visitors, regardless of their age, ability or background level. Her passion is science, and her conviction is that it can be enjoyed and studied by all, including people with disabilities.

Using a three-wheel scooter, Dr. Davidson moves about the Museum of Science planning and developing the science content for exciting new exhibits.

"'New England Habitats' was my first project at the Museum," Dr. Davidson describes. "It involved augmenting one of the museum's oldest exhibits, a beautiful old diorama hall with huge windows showing typical New England habitats, including seashore, lake shore, woodland, mountain, etc.

"The full-size scenes are of actual places in New England. The dioramas are, of course, behind glass. The additions were meant to bring the essence of each scene out in front of its window, with something to touch, something to smell, text labels that are easily seen and understood, and an audible label. The audio label described the scene and also included sounds that one might expect to hear in that particular habitat. My goal was to make the space an interesting and compelling place for everyone, including people who, for one reason or another, could not read text. The approach was to offer multisensory choices."

This project was so unique, serving as a model of what can be done in terms of accessibility, that its story is told in the book, *New Dimensions for Traditional Dioramas: Multisensory Additions for Access, Interest, and Learning*," written by Dr. Davidson and published by the Museum of Science in 1991.

"'Messages,'" Dr. Davidson describes another favorite exhibit, "is an exhibit about human communication. The exhibit theme is that people communicate in many different ways, and it isn't communication unless the receiver gets it.

"'Messages' is an interactive exhibit. There are a couple of videos, including one of *Little Red Riding Hood*, in which the story is communicated by using American Sign Language (ASL). Another video is of a group of kids who are deaf interviewing a group of elders who are deaf. Still another video is the story told by a group of World War II veterans – the Navajo Indian code talkers. As U.S. Marines, they developed and used a Navajo language-based code that the Japanese were never able to crack.

"All the other components of the exhibit are activities. For example, there's an activity where people can smell smoke, hear a siren, and see a flashing red light, and are asked what those three things communicate to them, possibly fire?

"Exhibit visitors can also listen to a few choices of background music and are asked which they think best fits a movie scene which is being audio described for those who cannot see the movie.

"Or the visitor can sit opposite another player with a curtain in between. Player number one builds a simple structure with variously shaped building blocks, and describes what he or she is doing to player number two, who tries to duplicate the structure without seeing it. How effective is player number one's communication skills?

"These activities, plus many more, keep the museum visitors of all ages entertained and learning for hours."

Dr. Davidson is helping to eliminate those "Not-for-you" messages that she heard during her childhood and adolescence and that so many young people still hear today. "Messages like that are incredibly destructive for the life of a child," Dr. Davidson says.

When asked what she believes is the key to her success, Dr. Davidson is quick to answer, "Persistence! I believe you have to just plow ahead with what you want to do. Don't let anyone tell you that you can't do it. The chances are – if you want to do something – you are capable of doing it. I know for myself, I have never wanted to be an ice-skating champion or even put on a pair of ice skates. That's not where my abilities lie. I have always known that I would find a way to do whatever I want to do, but I would have to rely on myself to get there. I can't imagine giving up. I'm too stubborn!

"The world is still full of gatekeepers, but now it's also full of people to inspire you and believe in you. These people will help you to find your strengths and interests and achieve your goals. And now there are technological tools out there to make it easier. Your job is to scoot around the gatekeepers, find people who support you, and then persevere."

"We have begun to ensure a future for ourselves, and a future for the millions of young people with disabilities, who I think will find a new world as they begin to grow up. Who may not have to suffer the kinds of discrimination that we have suffered in our own lives. But that if they do suffer it, they'll be strong and they'll fight back.

"And that's the greatest example, that we, who are considered the weakest, the most helpless people in our society, are the strongest, and will not tolerate segregation, will not tolerate a society which sees us as less than whole people. But that we will together, with our friends, reshape the image that this society has of us.

"We are no longer asking for charity. We are demanding our rights!

"We are victorious. We are strong. And we will march ahead together. And nothing will stop our achieving equal opportunity, and the right to move about freely in this society."

–Ed Roberts, leader of the disability rights Movement

Excerpts taken, with permission, from Ed Roberts's 504 Victory Speech, delivered on April 30, 1977.

www.wid.org/news/celebrating-a-disability-rights-milestone-ed-roberts-504-victory-speech

19
Surround Yourself with Smart People
David H. Pierce

Performing magic tricks, reading comic books, and playing sports filled much of David's leisure time when he was growing up. Above all, though, his favorite childhood hobby was shooting films with a home movie camera.

"My love affair with media began when I was five years old," David remembers. "In 1970 I got a Kenner Easy-Show movie projector. I was fascinated with the films that were silent because they had subtitles."

David spent many long hours watching these films and reading the printed text as it popped up on the bottom of the screen. "It was great," he said, "because with these subtitles I now knew what the characters in the films were saying."

David was born in Niagara Falls, New York, on July 2, 1965. He was born profoundly deaf. It is believed that his mother may have contracted rubella, also known as German or three-day measles, when she was pregnant with him.

David's four-year-old sister, his only sibling at that time, was thrilled to hear she was getting a little brother. But they would have only a short time together. One year later, in 1966, David's sister was diagnosed with croup, a childhood illness which, in the 1960s, was associated with diphtheria, a respiratory infection. At that time, croup was often fatal. Sad to say, this was the case for David's older sister. She died when she was just four years old.

David was much too young to realize the heartbreak that had befallen his parents. But when David was six years old, the Pierce family would welcome a new life into the family, a baby sister for David who, as she grew, would look to her older brother for entertainment with his magic shows and homemade movies.

"I started off by collecting and editing films," David recalls, "and then, when I was around eight years old, I started shooting my own films. One thing for sure is that my parents encouraged me to take interest in films, magic, and comic books as hobbies. They bought me movie equipment for me to play with and when I visited my grandfather, who was in Massachusetts and Florida, I saw his photo and film work which quite fascinated me. I could never have enough of it and would see them over and over again. He started shooting movie films in the 1930s, and it was fascinating seeing my father as a little boy. My grandfather, like my father, was an engineer by profession, and was an exceptionally gifted photographer and filmmaker, and was a great inspiration to me."

It was also at age eight that David moved with his family to Grand Island, located between Buffalo and Niagara Falls, New York, where David continued attending public school.

Remembering his early school years, David said, "My greatest challenge during those years was trying to make my speech understandable to my hearing peers. I did not learn sign language until I was nineteen years old. It took me several years to get my speech to a decent, understandable level."

He practiced pronouncing consonants, forming vowels with his lips, using his tongue to help speak words, spending countless hours working at something that every one of his classmates could do without applying one bit of effort.

"What did you say?" was often the response that his speech drew from both classmates and teachers. "Try again" and "I don't understand what you're saying" were coupled with stares and sometimes cruel laughter as David attempted to interact using the form of communication that everyone else around him understood, the spoken word.

"He sounds different and this can only mean one thing," many of his classmates and even some adults, concluded. "He must not be very smart."

"I knew I was smarter than they were," David affirms his intelligence. "And so I discarded their comments outright. I often had to help other students with their poor writing skills, which made me realize that it was an educational issue rather than an audiological issue."

Not everyone, however, questioned David's IQ. He had many close, supportive friends who knew his difficulty with speech was due to his inability to hear and not to a lack of understanding.

Give up? No way!

"It's not in my nature to quit," David professes. "There is no other option than to succeed."

As David entered junior high school, and later high school, he took with him his enjoyment of sports. Joining both the track and gymnastic teams at school, David made lasting and valuable friendships with his teammates and also went on to earn JV and varsity letters in both sports.

"Another thing that was important in growing up," David remembers, "was my involvement in Boy Scouts and Explorers. My dad, who is the recipient of the Silver Beaver Award, a very high honor in scouting, was a scouter for many years, and was scoutmaster and Explorer advisor when I was involved. Scouting helped me to be well-rounded. I went the full cycle from Cub Scouts in elementary school to Explorers in high school, earning my Star Scout badge."

David has a lot of fun memories from his time spent in Explorers, from the fifty-mile canoe trip at age fifteen to the whitewater rafting trip two years later. As David entered his junior year of high school, he left Explorers and joined his high school's gymnastics team. High school sports kept David busy, but sports was merely an enjoyable past time; it was not what he was passionate about.

Coming from a family of engineers, it would not have been surprising had David chosen engineering as his career. "But I was terrible in math and so I went into television and film instead of following in the family tradition," David says. And rightfully so, because his passion, his absolute allegiance, was working with film production.

Since captioned television wasn't widely available during David's childhood, he relied on subtitles. But subtitles only translate the spoken word. Captions, on the other hand, provide more detailed information to a television or movie viewer who cannot hear, such as the identity of speakers and their tone of voice, along with a description of music or sound effects being used.

David was six years old when captioning was first previewed to the public in 1971 at the First National Conference on Television for the Hearing Impaired in Nashville, Tennessee. But more work needed to be done. David would be seventeen years old before captioning was available for television shows happening in real-time, such as the news or sports events.

Technology was beginning to make media more accessible to people with hearing impairments. In 1983, David, now eighteen years old, got his first closed caption decoder to help him stay on top of the latest advances as they were happening.

His fascination with film production had been cultivated over the years. As he graduated from high school, David was prepared to immerse himself in studying and working in the field he had loved since childhood. He entered college at the National Technical

Institute for the Deaf (NTID) in Rochester, New York, with a major in media technologies.

"I was nineteen years old when I entered college and this was when I began learning sign language," David said. "When I was in college at NTID, I ran the student television network as its executive director. That experience eventually led me to run a 24/7 national cable television network after graduation from college. I oversaw 49,000 hours of national satellite broadcasts in fifteen million households nationwide."

David's childhood dream was coming true.

While earning a degree in media technologies, David teamed up with David B. Strom to form Davideo Productions in 1986. They produced television programming for local clients in Rochester. David graduated in February of 1988, and four months later, in June, Davideo Productions was shut down when David was hired at Silent Network in Los Angeles, a cable TV network for viewers who are deaf.

In 1990, Silent Network was sold to San Antonio, Texas investors and David moved to San Antonio to continue its operation.

"Then on July 26, 1990, when the Americans with Disabilities Act (ADA) was passed," David explains, "America's Disability Channel was born to serve as a media conduit for issues related to people with disabilities. I was one of the founding members of that network. Two networks, Silent Network and America's Disability Channel, ran on national satellite until 1994, when the owners decided to merge the two into one network, Kaleidoscope Television. In April 1995, KTV was launched as a 24/7 network."

Mr. Pierce worked his way up to vice president of programming and operations for KTV. He was on the team that built this national cable television network from the ground up, running it twenty-four hours a day, seven days a week, with captioning for 100% of their programs, making it totally accessible to the deaf community in fifteen million households nationwide.

Mr. Pierce is also the inventor of an editing technique known as the Pierce Method for Deaf Editors, which allows editors who have a hearing loss to cut video to audio. Mr. Pierce gained experience and knowledge during his years with KTV that would prepare him for even bigger things to come.

Mr. Pierce explains, "KTV filed for chapter seven bankruptcy and closed its doors in November 2000. In December 2000, I re-launched Davideo Productions as a sole proprietorship based in Seguin, Texas."

Davideo Productions is a broadcast television and motion picture film production, syndication and consulting firm of which Mr. Pierce is the owner and chief executive officer. He is also the co-owner and managing partner of Sign City Television, LLC, a programming service for national broadcasts targeted to viewers who are deaf and hard of hearing. And if that's not enough, there are still more exciting ventures that keep Mr. Pierce busy.

Remember the kids in school who teased David for his different communication skills? Well today, successful businessman David Pierce has the last laugh. He's the creator of a comic strip called *The Old Fogeys*. "It's a comic strip that I write and draw weekly," Mr. Pierce explains. "Created in 2001, it focuses on deaf issues and concerns."

Through *The Old Fogeys*, Mr. Pierce questions, in a fun way, the lack of understanding the hearing world has of people who are deaf. An example of this would be the comic strip, based on a true experience, about a waitress offering Braille menus to customers who are deaf.

The Old Fogeys is published every week through the international deaf and hard of hearing electronic newsletter, *Deaf Digest*, which can be found at www.DeafDigest.com

Mr. Pierce has been included in *Who's Who in the Media and Communications*, and was named one of the Top 10 People in 1997 by Hearing Health magazine.

"I'd like to continue to make an impact by providing broadcast television programming for the benefit of deaf and hard of hearing people, promote unity among deaf media professionals, and help increase the number of motion picture films for deaf and hard of hearing people," Mr. Pierce says.

Looking back on David's childhood, who could have guessed that this young boy who was often teased for his different communication skills would one day grow up to be honored and recognized for making an impact in broadcast television programming and motion picture films, a media used to communicate to millions of people around the world!

"The main key to my success," Mr. Pierce reveals, "has been perseverance and surrounding myself with smart people who have a successful business background. To succeed," Mr. Pierce continues, "know what your abilities are and do everything you can to maximize them. If you want to do something, do it. Don't listen to naysayers as they are the ones who are not smart enough to figure a way to work around whatever disability they perceive you to have. Be the best you can be and never stop learning."

For more information about David H. Pierce and his companies, visit www.davideo.tv and www.SignCity.tv.

"**At first dreams seem impossible, then improbable, then inevitable.**"

– Christopher Reeve

www.ChristopherReeve.org

20
I Took Advantage of Every Opportunity Thrown at Me
Erik Weihenmayer

"Reach higher, Erik. Left hand up another six inches. That's good. Keep going. Higher. Reach higher."

Sixteen-year-old Erik was attempting to do something he had never tried before – rock climbing. Ever since he had heard about the sport, he was curious. Could this be something he could do?

He said, "Unlike a basketball or football which is always moving, a mountain is standing still." But why would this be important to a teenaged boy?

Erik was born on September 23, 1968, in Princeton, New Jersey. A few months after Erik was born, his father noticed that Erik's eyes shook when tracking the football that he was passing in front of him. So began a nightmare of doctor visits trying to find an explanation. Finally, when Erik was just two years old, he and his parents arrived at the famed Boston eye clinic, Retina Associates.

"Your son," the ophthalmologist explained to Erik's parents, "has an eye disorder called retinoschisis. It's an eye disease which is characterized by the abnormal splitting of the neurosensory layers of the retina in both eyes. Erik will be totally blind by his early teens."

Erik, using very thick glasses to see to read, was accepted into a private school on the condition that his mother attend school with him to help him. Eventually she backed away so Erik could become more independent.

His dad, a former U.S. Marine and Vietnam veteran, was relentless about finding adaptations for every outdoor activity that Erik showed interest in. His mother, just as determined and very creative, read his school assignments to him as well as his Cub Scout manuals.

As Erik grew, his eyesight worsened. One day, Erik's mother found her thirteen-year-old son crying. It was the day eye doctors had said would arrive, but Erik had always hoped they would be wrong.

"I can't see anything," Erik said through his tears. "I can't do sports. I'm not going to have any friends. Forget girlfriends. I hate this. I hate everything."

His mother's words tried to comfort him. "I see so much for you, more than you and I can ever imagine. You're going to have the most extraordinary life."

Erik entered his freshman year of high school, now totally blind. His school books were brailed but he wasn't a proficient Braille reader.

"Read this," his Braille instructor insisted as she handed Erik a page of Braille. He ran his fingers across the top of the page. It made no sense to him. He heard the teacher's frustrated sigh as she reached over and turned the page right side up. He wondered, "How am I ever going to learn this? I can't even tell when the page is upside down."

At lunch time, Erik sat by himself as he listened to conversations going on all around him, wishing he could join in on the debates about his favorite sports teams. His fifteen-year-old mind cried out for freedom, the freedom that sight gave to his peers. He saw blindness as his enemy, the thief that had stolen his independence.

In time, however, Erik realized that going blind had actually set him free. Prior to going blind, he couldn't participate in contact sports for fear an impact would sever his retina nerve. With no sight left to lose, this was no longer a concern. He tried out for the wrestling team at his high school. Despite weighing only 114 pounds, he lasted longer than any other boy when wrestling the captain during freshman tryouts.

The next summer, Erik went off to wrestling camp. At the end of the first week, Erik called home with the exciting news of how well he had done. Both thrilled and relieved, his parents assured him that they would be at the big camp-ending tournament the following Saturday.

Two days before the tournament, however, Erik's dad arrived at the wrestling camp. "Erik," his dad began slowly, "I'm sorry, there's no other way to tell you this. There's been a terrible car accident. Your mom's been killed."

"If I had gone blind a thousand times," Erik said, "the pain would have been nothing in comparison. How could it be? The person who had savagely protected me all my life was gone. I was beginning to regain myself after blindness. Just as I began to know that blindness could not kill my hope or happiness, another blow, twice as devastating as the first, had slapped me down again."

Fortunately, he was getting pretty good in wrestling, making new friends, and he was finally, with the unrelenting support of his Braille instructor, becoming a proficient Braille reader.

One afternoon, Erik read in a Braille newsletter about a summer program at The Carroll Center for the Blind located in Newton, Massachusetts. He was curious. He had never met other blind kids and he wondered if they would be like him. Erik's dad signed him up for the two-week program.

The days were filled with learning new technologies, fun outings, swimming, horseback riding, and finally, the last four days were devoted to rock climbing, the whole reason Erik had chosen to attend.

When it was Erik's turn to attempt a climb, he tied the knot to his harness the way the instructor had shown. "Reach up to find the next hold," the instructor called out as Erik began slowly moving up the rocks. After just a few minutes, Erik had the hang of it and began moving faster than anyone else. He was hooked. This was a sport he could become passionate about.

Later that summer, Erik had another wonderful surprise. He received his first guide dog from Fidelco Guide Dog Foundation, located near Hartford, Connecticut. Wizard was a sleek, black and tan German shepherd who went everywhere with Erik, including to high school as Erik began his junior year.

Wizard was especially popular with Erik's guidance counselor. "She would keep a bowl of water in her office for Wizard," Erik described, "and would even drive us to the vet when Wizard was sick."

"She also did a lot for me," Erik continued. "She connected with the human side. She said she saw a lot of kids in high school who encountered very difficult times. But she also saw them grow up and become very successful. She told me, "You're going to do great."

Erik said, "You have no idea when you're a kid if you're going to make it, if you'll ever figure it out, find the right answers."

During Erik's senior year in high school, he was figuring things out. The school's wrestling captain, he represented the state in the National Freestyle Wrestling Championships.

In 1987, Erik graduated from Weston High School in Connecticut and was accepted to Boston College.

"During my freshman year," Erik describes, "I was diagnosed with glaucoma in my left eye. It was very painful and finally the eye had to be removed. I was shaking as they wheeled me into the operating room."

One summer, he decided he would look for an off-campus job. In addition to managing a weight room and giving tours on campus, Erik was now a certified scuba diver. His resume looked great. But he was turned down for every job he applied for, including a job to be a dishwasher at a restaurant.

"They may not tell you directly that you're not going to amount to anything," Erik said, "but they lower their expectations because they don't know what's possible, because so few people ever push the envelope. They gave me many reasons why I wasn't hired. Some of them made me wonder, are they right? When you haven't been given the chance to prove them right or wrong, you just don't know. That's the tricky part. You're not given the license to stumble and fail.

"It's important to find people who believe in what you might be able to do," Erik continues. "When I learned other sports, like paragliding and ice climbing, it was because someone said, 'Let's try it. I'll help.' They would say, 'We'll figure it out together.'"

After graduating from college, now twenty-two years old, he worked on his master's at night at Lesley College in Cambridge, working as an assistant teacher during the day.

Upon completing his Master's degree in middle school education in 1993 from Lesley College, Erik decided it was time for a new adventure. He applied for and was hired at the Phoenix Country Day School, a prestigious private school in Arizona.

Erik and Wizard greeted their sixth graders on the first day of school. "I had to do some things differently from my sighted colleagues," Erik said. "Some things I tried worked, some did not.

One thing for sure is that my students were given more responsibility than they probably had in other classrooms."

Teaching English and math to fifth graders was rewarding, but there were two bonuses that even Erik had not counted on. Both would change his life forever. First, he met Ellen, a sixth grade teacher. It wasn't long before even Wizard noticed the strong attraction between the two and began taking Erik straight to Ellen any time he saw her at school. Erik and Ellen soon fell in love.

The second bonus was making a new friend who would challenge Erik to reach higher than even he may have first believed to be possible. Sam, a substitute teacher at the school, mentioned to Erik one day that he was going to the gym to do some rock climbing. Erik said he would join him. They began working out together several nights a week at the Phoenix Rock Gym and on local rock faces.

One afternoon, while out doing a rock climb, Sam suggested they do something a little more challenging. He suggested Mount McKinley in Alaska. "You're joking, right?" Erik answered, thinking Sam had lost his mind. There was a big difference between Mount McKinley, the highest peak in North America, and the rock faces they had been climbing in the desert. Despite how ridiculous this idea first sounded, Erik wondered, "Could we really do it?"

Believing they could, they began a two-year training regimen, first doing more challenging rock climbs in the desert. When they couldn't get to the mountains every day, they continued their training by running up and down fifty flights of stairs at the tallest building in downtown Phoenix. They were each wearing a seventy-pound backpack to simulate what it would be like on the climb.

They first attempted to climb Mount Rainier in Washington State. They did not succeed due to harsh weather. Next, they attempted to climb Longs Peak in Colorado. It was extremely brutal, with 100-mile-an-hour winds. Once again, they did not summit. Despite these two so-called failures, they had learned a lot and were convinced that if they could survive those two mountains, they could summit McKinley.

With the American Foundation for the Blind sponsoring the Mount McKinley expedition, Erik and Sam began the climb in early June of 1995. They summitted on June 27, Helen Keller's birthday.

Erik began to have a dream. He said, "I even dreamed about a greater challenge, one so immense I didn't even speak it aloud for fear of sounding ridiculous."

He had read a book called *Seven Summits*, by Dick Bass, in which the author talked about climbing the highest peak on each of the seven continents. Erik's inner voice began speaking to him, saying, "Hold on there, you've climbed one big mountain. Let's not get carried away."

By the time he returned home from the McKinley climb, Erik knew he wanted Ellen to be in his life forever. He proposed to her and she said yes. Erik and Ellen were married at 13,000 feet on the Shira Plateau on Mount Kilimanjaro, the highest peak on the African continent. His dad and a few friends were there to celebrate. The following day, Erik continued the climb, reaching the highest peak on the second of the seven continents.

Mount Aconcagua, the highest peak in South America, would be Erik's third expedition, sponsored by the Glaucoma Research Foundation, an organization committed to both glaucoma research and prevention. Despite intense pain from the glaucoma in his remaining eye, Erik and his team summitted Aconcagua in late December of 1998, following a failed attempt the year prior.

As the school year came to a close in May of 1999, Erik made the decision to leave his six-year teaching career to devote all his time to mountain climbing. Already a pioneer in this sport, Erik's calendar was also filled with speaking engagements as he shared valuable lessons he had learned with corporations, universities, and youth audiences.

In January of 2000, Erik's other eye had to be removed as a result of the glaucoma. As sad as this was, there was nothing that could diminish the joy that came into Erik and Ellen's life six months later when their baby girl was born.

A few months after baby Emma was born, Erik's dad announced some incredible news – the National Federation of the Blind would fund Erik's expedition to summit Mount Everest, the highest mountain on Earth. Erik's dad said, "If Erik can get to the summit, it won't just change people's attitudes about what blind people can do, it will shatter them."

On May 25, 2001, Erik did shatter those attitudes as he became the first person who is blind to summit Mt. Everest.

How did a child who had endured so many heartaches, failures, and self-doubt, grow up to reach the top of the world as an adult?

"There's no way to make your life into an adventure unless you can take advantage of every opportunity that's thrown in front of you," Erik explains. "If I had gotten this Braille newsletter that talked about taking blind kids rock climbing and had made excuses and not taken action on it, my whole life would have been different. The only reason I became a climber is because I said yes. I didn't know if I would like it, but I said yes.

"I took advantage of every opportunity thrown at me. Don't build walls around you. Try new things. One of those things might be the thing that will catapult your life. You can make yourself into whatever you want to become. It starts with you being willing. Open yourself up to new experiences. You have a choice every time adversity hits you. You can be destroyed by it, or you can harness its energy and learn to grow and become more innovative because of it.

"Inside each of us is something I can only describe as a light, which has the capacity to feed on adversity, to consume it like fuel. When we tap into that light, every frustration, every setback, every obstacle becomes a source to power our lives forward. The greater the challenge, the brighter the light burns. Through it, we become more focused, more creative, and more driven, and can even learn to transcend our own perceived limitations to bring our lives more purpose and power."

On August 20, 2008, Erik's dream of climbing the seven summits – the highest mountain on each of the seven continents – became a reality, joining fewer than 100 mountaineers who have accomplished this feat.

Also in 2008, Erik and Ellen welcomed their second child, a son, into their family. Arjun Lama came to the U.S. from Nepal after a long struggle to adopt him.

To see Erik Weihenmayer in action, visit www.youtube.com/watch?v=JnR2dpLnS14.

For teacher and student resources about blindness, geography, and mountain climbing, visit www.ClimbingBlind.org.

For more information about Erik, including his books, DVD, and videos, visit www.TouchTheTop.com.

Excerpts taken, with permission, from Erik's book, *Touch the Top of the World,* and his DVD with the same title.

A Note from the Publisher

Together we can change attitudes about people with disabilities.

We invite you to keep in touch with Prove Them Wrong and author Nancy Shugart.

Sign up for the free Prove Them Wrong Ezine and join us on your favorite social media sites by visiting our website.

At our website, you can also learn how to use this book to raise money for your favorite non-profit organization.

Visit www.ProveThemWrong.com.

Tell Us Your Story

We're looking for stories for our future Prove Them Wrong books. Do you have a story of persistence when others thought you should just give up?

We are looking for personal stories that teach an important lesson about the value of never giving up. If you believe you have such a story, then visit www.ProveThemWrong.com and tell us your story!

About the Author

After going blind at age eight, Nancy Shugart grew up to accomplish something that many had said would be impossible for her to achieve. She lived her dream as a public school teacher, teaching in the Austin Independent School District in Austin, Texas for twenty-one years.

Today she is an author, speaker, and businesswoman. In addition to this book, she is the author of the book, *Challenged to Win*, which tells her personal story, and is the author of the DVD, *Align Your Dreams with Your Power*.

Nancy is the founder and owner of Prove Them Wrong, a company whose mission is to provide evidence of what happens when children, teens, and adults have the courage to refuse to quit.

To learn more about Nancy Shugart and her company, visit www.ProveThemWrong.com.

Resources

Abilicorp
2002 Addison Street, Suite 201
Berkeley, CA 94704
510-654-4263
www.Abilicorp.com

Ability Magazine
949-854-8700
www.AbilityMagazine.com

AdLit.org
Adolescent Literacy
WETA Public Television
2775 S. Quincy St.
Arlington, VA 22206
703-998-2600
www.AdLit.org

Amazing Video Magnifiers
866-733-5157
CustomerService@AmazingVideoMagnifiers.com
www.AmazingVideoMagnifiers.com

American Association of Intellectual and Developmental Disabilities
800-424-3688
www.AAMR.org

American Council of the Blind
2200 Wilson Boulevard
Suite 650
Arlington, VA 22201
800-424-8666
www.ACB.org

American Foundation for the Blind
800-232-5463
afbinfo@afb.net
www.afb.org

American Sign Language Teachers Association
www.ASLTA.org

American Speech-Language-Hearing Association
301-296-5700
actioncenter@asha.org
www.ASHA.org

America's Promise Alliance
1110 Vermont Avenue, N.W.
Suite 900
Washington, DC 20005
202-657-0600
www.AmericasPromise.org

Association for Education & Rehab of Blind & Visually Impaired
703-671-4500
www.AERBVI.org

Boy Scouts of America
www.scouting.org

BrainLine.org
Traumatic Brain Injury & Head Injury Resource
WETA Public Television
2775 S. Quincy St.
Arlington, VA 22206
703-998-2020
www.BrainLine.org

Canine Companions for Independence
866-224-3647
www.canineCompanions.org

Chamber of Commerce for Persons with Disabilities, Inc.
6932 Sylvan Woods Drive
Sanford, FL 32771
info@DisabilityChamber.org
www.DisabilityChamber.org

Children's Seashore House of the Children's Hospital of Pennsylvania
www.CHOP.edu

Christopher and Dana Reeve Foundation
800-225-0292,
www.ChristopherReeve.org

Council for Exceptional Children
703/264-9415
www.cec.sped.org

Disaboom, Inc.
info@Disaboom.com
www.Disaboom.com

Easter Seals, Inc.
233 South Wacker Drive
Suite 2400
Chicago, IL 60606
www.EasterSeals.com

Enable America, Inc.
P.O. Box 3031
Tampa, FL 33601
877-362-2533
www.EnableAmerica.org

Epilepsy Foundation of America
www.EpilepsyFoundation.org

Equal Opportunity Publications, Inc.
445 Broad Hollow Road
Suite 425
Melville, NY 11747
631-421-9421
www.EOP.com

Fidelco Guide Dog Foundation,
860-243-4800
www.fidelco.org

Glaucoma Research Foundation
800-826-6693
question@glaucoma.org
www.glaucoma.org

Goodwill Industries International, Inc.
15810 Indianola Drive
Rockville, MD 20855
800-741-0186
www.Goodwill.org

Guide Dogs for the Blind
800-295-4050
www.GuideDogs.com

Hearing Health Magazine
212-328-9480
info@drf.org
www.DRF.org

Hire Disability Solutions
327 Ridgewood Avenue
Paramus, New Jersey 07652
800-238-5373
www.HireDS.com

International Dyslexia Association
410-296-0232
www.interDys.org

LD OnLine
WETA Public Television
2775 S. Quincy St.
Arlington, VA 22206
ldonline@weta.org
www.LDOnline.org

Learning Store
P.O. Box 2284
So. Burlington, VT 05407
800-757-6845
www.LearningStore.org

March of Dimes
914-997-4488
www.MarchOfDimes.com

MS Musing
www.MSMusings.com

Muscular Dystrophy Association
800-572-1717
www.MDA.org

National Association for Parents of Children with Visual Impairments
800-562-6265
napvi@perkins.org
www.NAPVI.org

National Association of the Deaf
www.NAD.org

National Autism Association
877-622-2884
naa@nationalautism.org
www.NationalAutismAssociation.org

National Dissemination Center for Children with Disabilities
NICHCY
1825 Connecticut Ave. NW
Suite 700
Washington, DC 20009
800-695-0285
www.NICHCY.org

National Education Association
202-833-4000
www.NEA.org

National Federation of the Blind
410-659-9314
www.NFB.org

National Meningitis Association
866-366-3662
support@nmaus.org
www.NMAUS.org

National MS Society
800-344-4867
www.NationalMSSociety.org

National Organization of Parents of Blind Children
www.NOPBC.org

National PTA
800-307-4782
info@pta.org
www.PTA.org

Pacer Center, Inc.
8161 Normandale Blvd.
Bloomington, MN 55437
888-248-0822
www.Pacer.org

Parent to Parent USA
www.P2PUSA.org

Prove Them Wrong
866-733-5157
info@ProveThemWrong.com
www.ProveThemWrong.com

Reading Rockets
WETA Public Television
2775 S. Quincy St.
Arlington, VA 22206
703-998-2001
www.ReadingRockets.org

Shriners Hospitals for Children
813-281-0300
www.ShrinersHQ.org

Texas Scottish Rite Hospital for Children
www.tsrhc.org

The Arc (advocacy, resources, & connections)
800-433-5255
administration@thearc.org
www.TheARC.org

United Cerebral Palsy
800-872-5827.
www.UCP.org

World Institute on Disability
510-763-4100
wid@wid.org
www.WID.org

www.ingramcontent.com/pod-product-compliance
Lightning Source LLC
Chambersburg PA
CBHW031249290426
44109CB00012B/497